Back to the Bible

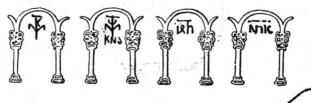

Frontispiece

A Page from the Gothic Gospels
(*Codex Argenteus*)
(St. Mark 7.3–6)

HOW OUR BIBLE CAME TO US

Its Texts and Versions

by

H. G. G. HERKLOTS
M.A.

NEW YORK
OXFORD UNIVERSITY PRESS
1954

Copyright 1954 by H. G. G. Herklots
Originally published in Great Britain
under the title Back to the Bible

Printed in Great Britain
at the Pitman Press · Belfast

PREFACE

WHEN I was invited to write a book on the general line of *how we got our Bible*, my inclination was to refuse. This was a job for experts. But later I was persuaded to attempt the task. There might be some advantage, I thought, in having a book written by a parish priest, in closer touch, perhaps, with the needs of ordinary Christians and the questions they are asking, than those who are engaged in full-time biblical study and research. Upon the work of these experts this book is everywhere dependent, as a continual series of footnotes will sufficiently indicate.

I should like to thank the Librarian of Doncaster Public Library for help in obtaining books which I did not possess.

H. G. G. HERKLOTS

Doncaster
St. Matthew's Day, 1953

CONTENTS

LIST OF ILLUSTRATIONS

Chapter One

WHICH BIBLE?

AT THE Coronation of Her Majesty Queen Elizabeth II, before the beginning of the Communion Service, she was given a book. This the Moderator of the General Assembly of the Church of Scotland received from the Dean of Westminster. As he presented it to the Queen seated in her Chair, the Archbishop of Canterbury used these words:

> *Our gracious Queen: to keep your Majesty ever mindful of the Law and the Gospel of God as the Rule for the whole life and government of Christian Princes, we present you with this Book, the most valuable thing that this world affords.*

Then the Moderator added:

> *Here is Wisdom; This is the royal Law; These are the lively Oracles of God.*

The book was, of course, a Bible.

What sort of Bible was it? The version most familiar to Englishmen; known by them as the Authorized Version, by Americans as the King James Version. Many of its words and phrases are so familiar that hearers almost imagine that it was in this stately language that the Bible itself was written. 'Charity suffereth long and is kind; charity envieth not; charity vaunteth not itself, is not puffed up, doth not behave itself unseemly, seeketh not her own, is not easily provoked, thinketh no evil . . .' The cadences have the ring of immortality: the assumption at the back of the mind is natural that they have been heard in Church so long as there has been a Bible to read or a Church to read it in. It is a little surprising to learn that they are a comparatively modern rendering of a rather less impressive Greek original.

The Authorized Version is the Bible which we take for granted: we are disturbed when translators in our own age render it differently. What are they doing to our Bible? we ask. It was good enough for our fathers. Surely it will do for ourselves and for our children?

When we make enquiries, however, we begin to discover that the Bible has not been nearly such a static thing as we imagined. It has worn all sorts of different dresses in different ages and countries. The Authorized Version dates from 1611 and is an astonishing production. The late Sir Arthur Quiller-Couch described it as a miracle, adding, for our greater astonishment, that it was a miracle produced by a committee of forty-seven men, 'not one of them known, outside of this performance, for any superlative talent'; and added further the comment of 'an old committee-man that this is not the way of committees—that only by a miracle is it the way of any committee.'[1] Despite this praise, and the praise which has been accorded to the Version by many generations of literary critics, it was not universally welcomed at its first appearance. It seemed modern and new-fangled. Some people still thought it dangerous that the Scriptures should be available to ordinary people at all and preferred that they should remain buried in the decent obscurity of Latin. What was good enough for their fathers was good enough for them. Others had already become used to another translation; most often the Geneva Bible which was produced by exiles during the reign of Queen Mary (1553–1558). This was of a smaller size than other Bibles of the time, so that it became the first popular family Bible. (Copies are still to be found in the hands of second-hand booksellers, who usually call it the 'Breeches Bible' because of its rendering of Genesis 3.7, 'they sewed figge tree leaves together, and made themselves breeches.')

The translators of the Authorized Version indeed felt it wise, in the manner of the time, to defend what they had done in a long introduction to the Book, entitled *The*

[1] *On the Art of Writing* (pocket edition, Cambridge, 1923), p. 108.

Translators to the Reader. From the opening sentences they cast themselves trenchantly about. 'Zeal to promote the common good, whether it be by devising any new thing ourselves, or revising that which hath been laboured by others, deserveth certainly much respect and esteem, but yet findeth but cold entertainment in the world. It is welcomed with suspicion instead of love, and with emulation instead of thanks: and if there be any hole left for cavil to enter (and cavil, if it do not find an hole, will make one), it is sure to be misconstrued, and in danger to be condemned.'[1]

The history of the Bible, considered as a book only, is one of constant innovation in lively conflict with a tenacious conservatism. Scholars gain fresh insights, which ordinary readers find disturbing, so that they reject or neglect them. Yet in the end the scholars win their way—except when it comes to singing. Anglican congregations still sing a version of the Psalms which is older than the Authorized Version. It is not a translation of the original Hebrew Psalms at all, but a translation of a translation; that is to say, it puts into English the Latin version of the Psalter with which congregations had been familiar for hundreds of years—as the Latin titles in the Prayer Book remind us. This version was made by a Yorkshireman from the North Riding, Miles Coverdale, and published in 1535. There have been suggestions in this century that it might be brought up to date; but nobody is in a hurry.

There are some other Biblical sentences in the Prayer Book which are older than the Authorized Version. The most famous are the Comfortable Words in the Communion Service, which first appeared in the earliest Prayer Book in 1549. 'Come unto me, all that travail and are heavy laden and I will refresh you' gives the meaning more exactly than 'I will give you rest'. The offertory sentences in the Communion Service are also from an earlier version—as the present writer discovered when he wished to preach from

---

[1] This Preface is not often printed in Bibles nowadays: but is available in an attractive popular edition issued by the Cambridge University Press.

the words 'While we have time, let us do good unto all men; and specially unto them that are of the household of faith', but could not discover them registered anywhere in his Concordance to the Holy Scriptures.

The Authorized Version was the culmination of a number of previous versions, the finest blossom on a flowering branch. The 'Englishing' of the Scriptures, as it was often called, had widespread national effects. In a famous passage in his *Short History of the English People*, John Richard Green declared, 'No greater moral change ever passed over a nation than passed over England during the years which parted the middle of the reign of Elizabeth from the meeting of the Long Parliament. England became the people of a book, and that book was the Bible. It was as yet the one English book which was familiar to every Englishman: it was read at churches and read at home, and everywhere its words, as they fell on ears which custom had not deadened to their force and beauty, kindled a startling enthusiasm.'[1] We may look back upon the process with some envy and some complacency: it is well to remember that the process was a costly one. Part of the cost had been paid before Elizabeth came to the throne, when William Tyndale was first strangled and then burned at Vilvorde in the Low Countries, in 1536.

Tyndale was at once the greatest hero in the story of modern Biblical translation and the greatest influence upon the style and diction of the Authorized Version. He was unable to complete the Old Testament; but what he had done was incorporated in later versions. His printed New Testaments—forbidden books in England from their first entry in 1525—were especially influential in fixing the phraseology of what was to follow. It has been calculated that even in the Revised Version of 1881 at least eighty per cent of the words stand precisely as they stood in Tyndale's Testament of 1525. Much therefore, of the Book which English sovereigns receive at their Coronation is taken from

[1] Opening of Ch. Eight.

PLATE I

S. Mathew.   Fo.vij.

blynge sake. Be ye not lyke them therfore. For youre father knoweth wherof ye have neade / before ye axe of him. After thys maner therfore praye ye.

Luc. xi. ¶O oure father / which art in heven halowed be thy name. Let thy kyngdome come. Thy wyll be fulfilled / as well in erth / as hit ys in heven. Geve vs this daye oure dayly breade. And forgeve vs oure treaspases / even as we forgeve them which treaspas vs. Lede vs nott in to tempracion. but delyver vs the from yvell / Amen. For and yf ye shall forgeve other men theyr

Math. viii. Mar. xi. treaspases / youre father in heven shall also forgeve you. But and ye will nott forgeve men there treaspases / no more shall youre father forgeve youre treaspases.

¶Moreovre when ye faste / be not sad as the ypocrytys are. For they disfigure there faces / that hit myght appere vnto men that they faste. Verely y say vnto you / they have there reward. But thou whe thou fastest / annoynte thyne heed / and wasshe thy face / that it appere not vnto men howe that thou fastest: but vnto thy father which ys in secrete: and thy father which seyth in secrete / shall rewarde the openly.

Lu. xii. ¶Gaddre not treasure to gether on erth / where ruste and mothtes corrupte / and where theves breake through and steale. But gaddre ye treasure to gyddre in heven / where nether ruste / nor yet mothtes corrupte: and where theves nether breake vppe / nor yet steale. For where soever youre treasure ys / theare are youre herttys also.

Luc. xi. ¶The light of thy body is thyne eye. Wherfore if thyne eye be *syngle / all thy body ys full of light. But and yf thyne eye be wycked / then is all thy body full of dercknes. Wherfore yf the light that ys in the be dercknes: howe greate ys that dercknes?

Lu. xvi. ¶No man can serve two masters. For other he shall hate the one / and love the other: or els he shall lene to the one / and despise that other. Ye cannott serve god and mammon. There accepteth fore y saye vnto you / be not carefull for youre lyfe what ye shall eate / or what ye shall dryncke / nor yet for youre boddy / what

Lu. xii. raymet ye shall weare. Ys not the lyfe more worth then meate: and the boddy moare of value then rayment? Beholde yes sake only.

Ꝺ iij

(marginal glosses)

es deserve ani thy / yng of god as a labourar deserueth hys hyre. For all good thynges come of the bounte / usnes / liberalite / mercy / promyses / trewth of goodi / the deseruinge of Christ bloud. olp but it ys a maner of spekinge, as we saye (thy labur or going was well rewarded) vnto hi that hath but fett only the promyses of a nodyr man.

*Syngle. The eye ising'e when a man i all his dedes loketh butt on the wil of god / z loketh nott for laude / honour or eni otherre war nother ascrybeth heven or a hyer roume therevnto.

as a thig purcha / sed bi the bloud of Christe / z worketh frely for lo /

(The Lutterworth Press)

A Page of St. Matthew (6.8–25) from Tyndale's
New Testament

(From *William Tyndale*, R. Demaus)

one formerly forbidden in the country by royal command. On the 4th of May, 1530, in the presence of Cardinal Wolsey, a great bonfire of these New Testaments was kindled in old St. Paul's Cathedral. Yet suppression could not be effective, now that the printing press was at work. The volumes came seeping through into the country from overseas. Tyndale's last recorded words were a loud cry, 'Lord, open the King of England's eyes.' His prayer was answered.

In 1538 the clergy of England received royal injunctions:

Item, that ye shall provyde . . . one boke of the whole Bible of the largest volume, in Englyshe, and the same sett up in summe convenyent place within the said churche that ye have cure of, whereas your parishners may most commodiouslye resort to the same, and rede yt; the charges of which boke shal be ratablie born between you the parson and the parishners aforsaid, that ys to say, the one half by yowe and th'other half by them.

Item, that ye discorage no man pryvely or apertly from the reading or hearing of the same Bible, but shall expresslye provoke, stere, and exhorte every parsone to rede the same, as that whyce ys the verye lively Worde of God that every Christen man ys bownde to embrace, beleve and followe, yf he loke to be saved; admonyshinge them neverthelesse to avoid all contention and altercation therein, and to use an honest sobrietye in the inquisition of the true sense of the same, and referre th'explication of obscure places to men of higher jugement in Scripture.

This introduced the first authorized version of the Scriptures, known as the Great Bible. It was indeed a book 'of the largest volume', a magnificent example of printing. Work on it was begun in Paris, where the best paper could be obtained. Then there came a mandate from the Inquisition forbidding the work. A portion was already in England. Many sheets were seized in France; but later 'four great dry vats full' were bought back from a haberdasher to whom they had been sold. Types, presses and men were brought over to England, and in April, 1539 the volume was completed. Its contents were based on earlier Bibles in which the work of Tyndale and Coverdale had been put together. This had been further revised by Coverdale. During the year the Bibles began to be set up in churches; and considerable numbers of people crowded around them to read, or, perhaps more often, to hear others read aloud.

Tyndale's work was unfinished. He had translated the New Testament from the Greek. He had translated the first five books of the Old Testament—the Pentateuch—and the Book of Jonah. He had also produced a translation of the 'Epistles taken out of the Old Testament, which are read in the Church after the Use of Salisbury' on certain Saints' days and other occasions. This was, in effect, an anthology from the Old Testament. It included extracts from the books of the Pentateuch, which he had already translated, and others from Proverbs, Isaiah, Jeremiah, Ezekiel, Joel, Hosea, Amos, Zechariah, and Malachi; as well as from Esdras, Wisdom and Ecclesiasticus, which are to be found in the Apocrypha.

He was not content. He had the burning zeal of scholar and evangelist combined. From his damp prison at Vilvorde he wrote to the Governor of the Castle, that

if I am to remain here during the winter, you will request the Procureur to be kind enough to send me from my goods which he has in his possession, a warmer cap, for I suffer extremely from cold in the head, being afflicted with a perpetual catarrh, which is considerably increased in this cell. A warmer coat also, for that which I have is very thin: also a piece of cloth to patch my leggings: my overcoat is worn out. He has a woollen shirt of mine, if he will be kind enough to send it. I have also with him leggings of thicker cloth for putting on above; he also has warmer caps for wearing at night. I wish also his permission to have a lamp in the evening, for it is wearisome to sit alone in the dark. *But above all, I entreat and beseech your clemency to be urgent with the Procureur that he may kindly permit me to have my Hebrew Bible, my Hebrew Grammar, and Hebrew Dictionary, that I may spend my time with that study.*[1]

We are reminded of St. Paul writing to Timothy from what was probably a much more hygienic imprisonment: 'The cloke that I left at Troas with Carpus, when thou comest, bring with thee, and the books, but especially the parchments.'[2] Tyndale was a modern translator because he went back, so far as he could, to the original documents in their original languages. Where did he get his Greek Testament from? How did he have a Hebrew Bible? These are questions to which we must turn in the next chapter.

[1] The original Latin of this letter, and a translation, are given in R. Demaus, *William Tyndale* (London, 1887) p. 437.

[2] 2 Timothy 4.13.

Chapter Two

BEHIND THE PRINTED NEW TESTAMENT

MANY Christian writers in recent years have been critical of the consequences of the Renaissance. They have condemned it as the source of much modern evil, especially of that pride and rebellion against God which has enabled man to feel that he is completely master in his own house. If Swinburne in the Nineteenth Century could write 'Glory to man in the highest, for man is the master of things' it was but the natural conclusion of a movement of thought reaching back to the Fifteenth. This feeling of self-sufficiency, we are told, began with the Renaissance, reached its climax in the Victorian Age, and is now coming to a sorry end. There is much truth in this analysis. Yet even Nicholas Berdyaev, the exiled Russian thinker to whom its formulation owes a great deal, recognised that the Renaissance was a movement within a Christian society and involving Christian presuppositions even when it was in rebellion against them.

Had there ever been known in man a creative urge so vigorous as was being shown in those first days of the Renaissance? Thus man affirmed his power to make freely, the liberty of his art. But he was still close to the spiritual wellsprings of life, not yet far on his way towards its surface. Renaissance man is a divided creature, belonging to two worlds, and it is this which makes the complexity and the richness of his creative power. The beginnings of the Renaissance can no longer be taken as merely a reproducing of antiquity, simply a return to paganism. There still remained to them many Christian elements and medieval principles, and a man so characteristic of the sixteenth century as Benvenuto Cellini, during the decline of the Renaissance, was not only a pagan but a Christian as well.[1]

There was a reaching back to antiquity and a reaching forward to the modern world. Yet even in the return to antiquity there was little that we should call antiquarian. Men went to the past as to the springs of new life. There developed a passionate search for manuscripts, in Latin, or, better still, in Greek, and the older the better. The clear thinking of classical authors would stimulate fresh thought for an age which was still to be made. The minds of Greece would enable men to shake off the fetters of an age which they had not yet learned to call medieval.

In the first place the return was to classical Greek: this stimulated a somewhat later return to the Greek of the New Testament. 'The study of Greek among the Italians appears, if we take the year 1500 as our standard, to have been pursued with extraordinary zeal. The youths of that day learned to speak the language, and half a century later, like the Popes Paul III and Paul IV they could still do so in their old age.'[2] This familiarity with Greek as a living language was made possible through the coming to Italy of many Greek refugees, on the move before the pressure of Turkish advance, which culminated in the fall of Constantinople in 1453. At the first, unfortunately, little use was made of this opportunity to gain fresh knowledge of the early days of the Christian Church. 'Exceptional opportunities for the furthering of Christian scholarship lay ready to the hands of the Italians in the fourteenth century; yet there is strikingly little to show that advantage was taken of them . . . The thought of applying the knowledge of Greek to the study of the Bible seems hardly to have occurred to the Italian scholars of the fourteenth century.'[3] As the Greek exiles became assimilated into Italian life the passion for their language and literature died away in Italy. But

[1] *The End of our Time* (Sheed & Ward, 1933) p. 18.
[2] Jacob Burckhardt, *The Renaissance in Italy* (fourth edition, 1898) p. 196.
[3] M. R. James, in *The Cambridge Modern History*, vol. i, p. 593.

already from Italy Northerners had caught the infection. Among them were some who realized that knowledge of Greek would give them a powerful lever for Church reform.

A desire for reform was widespread in the Church in the Fifteenth Century. It was in no sense confined to what are thought of as the countries of the Reformation. Considerable numbers of people were becoming convinced that the Church had taken a good many wrong turnings. The best way to get onto the right track would be by going the whole way back to the Church's starting place. There needed to be stripped from Christian practice and belief the more recent accretions by which its primitive purity had become corrupted. In this sense the movement of the Renaissance was one *against* paganism. Church reformers were as keen as any other people to get hold of old manuscripts; to find out what the early Fathers had said; to discover what the New Testament had conveyed to those for whom it was first written. *Back to the Bible* was in some ways a Renaissance motto.

The Bible which men had was in Latin. There was an advantage in this. Latin was understood by educated people from one end of Europe to another. In the past, however, not many people were educated apart from the clergy; and the clergy were not usually such experts as some of the laity supposed. Now education was spreading. More lay people read Latin; but the growth of education was the beginning of a tide which would demand literature in the new modern languages of French, Italian, English and German, and the Bible translated into them. Scholars began to ask questions about this Latin Bible. Was its text pure? Did it faithfully represent the Greek and Hebrew which lay behind it? Had it been altered through frequent copying? It was especially important to discover answers to these questions now that the printing press could multiply copies rapidly. It would be unfortunate if it only multiplied mistakes.

The work of copyists had always been important; and with the Renaissance their numbers had increased. In Italy there were the highly-skilled professional *scrittori*, who understood Greek, and the *copisti*, clerks, and schoolmasters picking up a little money on the side, as well as monks and nuns. All their work was graceful and beautiful; as indeed were the first printed books. At first, however, Italians laughed at the invention 'made among the barbarians in some German city.'[1] It was in 1454—the year after the fall of Constantinople—that Johann Gutenberg began to use movable type. In 1456 he issued the first book printed in Europe, a splendid Latin Bible. In Germany printing was welcomed by the Church. Indulgences were published for the benefit of those who bought and sold printed books. (Later on, printing was to produce a growth of ecclesiastical censorship.) Caxton began printing in England in 1474; and, though he started with a History of Troy and went on to *The Game and Playe of the Chesse*, he was soon printing religious works as well. One of these, his version of the Golden Legend, issued in 1483, contained a great part of the Bible.

The invention of printing brought a new attitude towards manuscripts. In some ways they became less important: it became old-fashioned to have books copied by hand: the *copisti* were on their way to becoming unemployed. For scholars, however, manuscripts were to acquire a new importance. They came to represent authority behind the printed page. They were searched out, copied, and compared. The very demand for them revealed the presence of old manuscripts which no one had seen for years. These were seen to be valuable. The process of discovery did not come to an end, but has rather increased, so that our knowledge to-day of the original New Testament is incomparably greater than that possessed by the men of the Renaissance.

The New Testament was written in Greek. Greek ideas had a great importance in the Middle Ages; but always at second-hand. 'All through the Middle Ages uneasy and

[1] Burckhardt, *op. cit.*, p. 194.

imperfect memories of Greece and Rome had haunted
Europe. Alexander, the great conqueror; Hector, the noble
knight and lover; Helen, who set Troy town on fire . . .
these phantoms, whereof the positive historic truth was lost,
remained to sway the soul and stimulate desire in myth and
saga.'[1] For the Middle Ages the Greek thinker, Aristotle,
was, in Dante's words, 'the master of them that know.'
Transformed and Christianised through its distillation in
the powerful mind of St. Thomas Aquinas, the thought of
Aristotle became the dominant factor in the creation of
Scholasticism, that medieval philosophy which aimed to
integrate all knowledge around theology, the Queen of the
sciences. Yet hardly anyone could read Aristotle in Greek.
In the Church the knowledge of Greek never quite died
out, but it was extremely rare. In the early days of the
English Renaissance it was thought that things were going
well because now five men in the country knew the language.

It was naturally to Italy that men turned who wished to
gain the new knowledge. They went to Italy to learn Greek
and to obtain any manuscripts which were available within
their means. Some found their way to Oxford and Cambridge. Scholars returned from across the Alps with a new
light in their eyes. In the Autumn of 1496 one of them, a
young man called John Colet, began to lecture at Oxford
on St. Paul's Epistle to the Romans. He spoke from the
Greek text. He paid little attention to traditional interpretations, to the notes which students had been taking down
for generations and learning by heart. He wanted to discover what St. Paul had meant when he first wrote. Colet
won many hearers. Before he left Oxford in 1505 to become
Dean Colet of St. Paul's, a younger man, William Tyndale,
had begun his studies at Oxford.

A scholar with a wider fame—though only thirty years old
at the time, the same age as Colet—was attracted to England
in 1498. This was a Dutchman, whose name Geert or
Gerard had been Latinized into Desiderius and Graecized

[1] J. A. Symonds, *Renaissance in Italy* (London, 1900), p. 38.

into Erasmus. A young English nobleman, Lord Mountjoy, who had been Erasmus' pupil in Paris and a generous benefactor to his impecunious teacher, persuaded him to cross the Channel. He did not know any English. This did not matter. His Latin would make him quickly at home among scholars. He came to learn, not English, but Greek. Two Englishmen, Grocyn and Linacre, had brought Greek from Italy, and Erasmus came to study under them. 'To belong to that little knot of men north of the Alps who already knew Greek—whose numbers might yet be counted on his fingers—this had now become his immediate object of ambition.'[1] In this ambition he succeeded. Later he spent about seven years at Cambridge, where he became both Lady Margaret Professor of Divinity and Professor of Greek. All the time he was working at the New Testament in both Greek and Latin, as well as upon the works of St. Jerome, himself the editor of the *Vulgate*, as the Latin Bible was called. It became known that Erasmus intended to produce an edition of the Greek New Testament with a fresh Latin translation alongside.

Here were two revolutionary proposals, the second, to the men of the time, probably more revolutionary than the first. To criticize the sacred Vulgate, to presume to improve upon St. Jerome, this was indeed to be an iconoclast. In March 1515 a sudden stimulus towards publication was given by a famous Swiss publisher, John Froben, who invited him to Basle to prepare a Greek New Testament upon the very lines on which he was working. Erasmus set off from England at once. Even on his way he had to meet criticisms of his project. His satirical *Praise of Folly* had already caused trouble enough. What would come next? An Open Letter from Martin Dorpius of the University of Louvain met him as he travelled:

> What matters it whether you believe or not that the
> Greek books are more accurate than the Latin ones;
> whether or not greater care was taken to preserve the sacred

[1] Frederic Seebohm, *The Oxford Reformers* (Everyman Library edition), p. 57.

books in all their integrity by the Greeks than by the Latins;—by the Greeks, forsooth, amongst whom the Christian religion was very often almost overthrown, and who affirmed that none of the Gospels were free from errors, excepting the one gospel of John. What matters all this when, to say nothing of anything else, the Church has continued throughout the inviolate spouse of Christ? . . . What if it be contended that the sense, as rendered by the Latin version, differs in truth from the Greek text? Then, indeed, adieu to the Greek. I adhere to the Latin because I cannot bring my mind to believe that the Greek are more correct than the Latin codices.'[1]

Erasmus could not accept any such forced good-bye. For him it was not adieu to the Greek, but welcome. He did not want to go part of the way back to the original New Testament but all the way.

How is it that Jerome, Augustine, and Ambrose all cite a text which differs from the Vulgate? How is it that Jerome finds fault with and corrects many readings which we find in the Vulgate? What can you make of all this concurrent evidence—when the Greek versions differ from the Vulgate, when Jerome cites the text, according to the Greek versions, when the oldest Latin versions do the same, when this reading suits the sense much better than that of the Vulgate—will you, treating all this with contempt, follow a version corrupted by some copyist? . . . In doing so you follow in the steps of those vulgar divines who are accustomed to attribute ecclesiastical authority to whatever in any way creeps into general use . . . I had rather be a common mechanic than the best of their number.'[2]

Basle was a centre of printing and a centre of learning. (The idea had hardly yet been born of printing other than learned books.) Here already great expense and care, and much time, had gone to the preparation and publication of

[1] Seebohm, *op. cit.*, p. 195, 196.   [2] *Ibid.*, p. 197.

PLATE II

(From a Seventeenth Century Dutch Engraving)

Erasmus at Work

(Note the filing system)

editions of St. Ambrose and St. Augustine. Erasmus, however, worked at great pressure, against the clock, as it
were. No doubt his publishers knew that another edition
of the Greek New Testament was being prepared in Spain
by Cardinal Ximenes. The Spanish edition was actually
printed first, but—owing to difficulties with the Inquisition
—it was not immediately published; so that Erasmus'
version is usually regarded as the first printed Greek New
Testament in Europe. It was issued on March 1st, 1516.

One of the Councils which endeavoured to reform the
Church from within had been held at Basle in 1431. To it
there had come a Dominican friar, John of Ragusa, who
later became a Cardinal. As a present to the Dominican
convent at which he had been lodged he left behind a
collection of books. Among these were three manuscripts of
parts of the New Testament in Greek. Others were added
to them. These—and two manuscripts lent by Dean Colet
from the library at St. Paul's—provided the basis for
Erasmus' edition. None of the manuscripts he used was
particularly old: one was almost new. None would be considered to-day to be authoritative for determining the text.
None was complete. But Erasmus used what he had and
got on with the job. He had no manuscript at all for the
last six verses of Revelation—the last page of an old book is
often apt to be missing—so he made his own translation
into Greek from the Latin!

Not many people had read the whole New Testament
even in Latin. There were customary passages which they
heard, to which customary interpretations were attached,
but little more. Now there was printed a volume containing
the whole New Testament as it was believed to have been
originally written, with a fresh Latin translation alongside.
The book was a best-seller. It is said that a hundred thousand
copies were sold in France alone. But it was not only the
sacred record which attracted buyers. It was also the Intro-
ductions which Erasmus wrote to the books; his Preface; and
his notes, which contained many sharply-barbed attacks

upon contemporary abuses. Thus on Matthew 23.27, in which Our Lord characterizes the Scribes and Pharisees as 'whited sepulchres', Erasmus wrote:

> What would Jerome say could he see the Virgin's milk exhibited for money, with as much honour paid to it as the consecrated body of Christ; the miraculous oil; the portions of the true cross, enough if they were collected to freight a large ship? Here we have the hood of St. Francis, there Our Lady's petticoat or St. Anne's comb, or St. Thomas of Canterbury's shoes; not presented as innocent aids to religion, but as the substance of religion itself—and all through the avarice of priests and the hypocrisy of monks playing on the credulity of the people. Even bishops play their part in these fantastic shows, and approve and dwell on them in their rescripts.[1]

Here was the spirit of the Renaissance at work in religion. In the Preface to the volume Erasmus struck the note of the new age:

> I wish that even the weakest woman should read the Gospel—should read the epistles of Paul. And I wish these were translated into all languages, so that they might be read and understood, not only by Scots and Irishmen, but also by Turks and Saracens. To make them understood is surely the first step. It may be that they might be ridiculed by many, but some would take them to heart. I long that the husbandman should sing portions of them to himself as he follows the plough, that the weaver should hum them to the tune of his shuttle, that the traveller should beguile with their stories the tedium of his journey.[2]

Erasmus' Greek Testament was the one used by Tyndale in making his translation into English—and in this way Erasmus' hope was fulfilled. When his commentary on the

---

[1] Quoted J. A. Froude, *Life & Letters of Erasmus* (Silver Library edition, 1910), p. 129.
[2] Seebohm, *op. cit.*, p. 203.

books was translated into English it was appointed by public authority to be placed in all our churches.

Cardinal Ximenes' production was on a larger scale. It is known as the Complutensian Polyglot: *Complutensian* from the Latin name of the University town of Alcala whence it originated: *polyglot* because in it there were set out Hebrew, Greek and Latin versions. The scholars who worked for Cardinal Ximenes are not thought to have had any really early manuscripts at their disposal.

Erasmus revised his work several times, and his last edition lay behind the Greek New Testament issued by Robert Étienne, or Stephanus, in Paris. The third Stephanus edition, issued in 1550, contained an important new addition. As well as the actual text there were printed a series of abbreviated notes indicating variations in the manuscripts used. This was the origin of the *critical apparatus*, which, with the wealth of documentary evidence now available, may take up more space on the printed page than the text itself.

Stephanus became a Protestant and migrated to Geneva. His next edition, issued there in 1551, was the first to contain numbered verses in the style which has since become customary, and which, in the hands of an uninstructed reader or speaker, may often lead to a distortion of the meaning. It is important for us nowadays to realize that, however useful the verse divisions may be, the actual authors neither thought nor wrote in verses. Theodorus Beza (or Theodore de Beze—as he was known to his friends) continued the work in Geneva. His edition published in 1582 used a Sixth Century manuscript which is known to scholars as *Codex Bezae*, or D. It is now at Cambridge. This work in Geneva had its influence in England, through the Geneva translation, prepared by exiles in the reign of Queen Mary (1553–1558) and first issued in 1560. This brought the verse divisions to England. The Geneva Bible was also the first to be printed in the simpler Roman type of to-day, as opposed to the old *black letter*, which was really an imitation of manuscript writing.

Meanwhile other printers were at work; and one of the Elzevir editions, published at Leyden in 1663, was to be extremely influential. It contained in its Preface these words: 'TEXTUM ergo habes, nunc ab omnibus RECEPTUM, in quo nihil immutatum aut corruptum damus.' ('You have therefore a TEXT, now RECEIVED by everyone, in which we give nothing deteriorated or corrupt.') TEXTUM RECEPTUM—the Received Text. The words seemed to act like a spell, to indicate that this really was an authorised version of the New Testament. New editions of the Greek Testament appeared; but they always took the fatally named *textus receptus* as their basis. Not until 1831 did a German scholar, Lachmann, construct a text entirely from ancient documents without the intervention of any printed edition. This began a new era in the history of the Biblical text, to which we shall refer in a later chapter.

The British and Foreign Bible Society continued to issue the Received Text of the Greek New Testament until 1904.[1] Yet it was based on the work of Erasmus, the Complutensian Polyglot, and a handful of manuscripts 'in fact, on something like a hundredth part of the Greek evidence now at our disposal, not to speak of versions and citations.'[2] So wrote Alexander Souter in 1925. The amount of evidence available to-day is greater, and some of it a good deal older. Until 1904, if you bought a Greek New Testament, it was likely to conclude with the six verses of Revelation which Erasmus rendered from Latin to Greek because he was in a hurry to beat a Spanish Cardinal and had no Greek manuscript for the verses available in Basle. Nevertheless, despite innumerable differences in detail, our modern knowledge has resulted in few *substantial* changes in the text of the New Testament. Through the hands of innumerable scribes and copyists it is substantially the same book which has been handed down.

---

[1] Since then they have issued the text of Eberhard Nestle. A new text is being prepared.
[2] *The Text and Canon of the New Testament* (Duckworth's Studies in Theology; second impression, 1925), p. 97.

Chapter Three

BEHIND THE PRINTED OLD TESTAMENT

A FASCINATING study might be made—by some encyclopaedic scholar—of the cultural and religious effects of dispersion, especially when it has been occasioned by persecution. Amongst refugees and emigrants there must always be an enforced value-judgment about their possessions. What things are to be left behind? What things are so precious that room must, at all costs, be found for them? (What things, also, are so light or small that they may be stowed away in some corner of the luggage?) Refugees have taken with them not only their prized personal possessions but their beliefs and their skills. It was with the persecution which began with the martyrdom of Stephen that the Christian Church began to prosecute its missionary task with vigour. 'They therefore that were scattered abroad went about preaching the word' (Acts 8.4). We have seen how Greeks fleeing before the Turkish invader helped to awaken classical interests in Italy. Compassionate Italians wanted to give these refugees a job. After all, they were Christians escaping from the power of the Infidel. What better than to employ them as teachers of their own language? In recent decades refugees from many countries have brought fresh life and skill to Britain and America. This has been to repeat a pattern familiar to history. British commercial enterprise owes a great deal to the Huguenots. Puritan exiles from England build up New England. But these were all dispersions limited in time and place. Throughout modern history there has, however, been one dispersed people *par excellence*. Into almost every nation the Jews have found their way.

Where they have entered they have brought their Sabbath and their Synagogue and their Scriptures. They have also brought their learning. 'At a period at which the vast majority of Europeans were illiterate, the Jews insisted as a religious duty upon a system of universal education of remarkable comprehensiveness. In every land to which they penetrated, schools of Rabbinical learning sprang up, in which the shrewd financiers became transmuted into acute scholars while their clients sat toping in their castles.'[1] If a western Christian wanted to learn Greek in the Middle Ages it was almost impossible. If he wanted to learn Hebrew there might, indeed, be social obstacles: but the books could be found, and men to teach the language. Thus the English- man, Stephen Harding (c. 1061–1134) Abbot of Cîteaux in Northern France, and founder of the Cistercian Order of monks, prepared a revised text of the Latin Bible for his monks, with the aid of some Jews, who helped him with the meaning of Hebrew words. In a copy of the original manu- script made in 1109 we read that 'I, Abbot Stephen, per- ceiving variations in the text in our books, visited certain Jews who were expert in their scripture, and I questioned them in the vernacular concerning all those passages in Scripture . . . In my presence these Jews turned to their numerous books, and, as I asked them, so they expounded to me in the vernacular the Hebrew or Chaldaean readings.'[2] The Abbot had been invited into a Rabbinical college. By 'Chaldaean' he meant what we call Aramaic, the language of the people in Palestine in the time of Jesus.

For some in the Middle Ages the Hebrew language itself, with its letters so different from those to which they were accustomed, and its 'wrong-way-round' way of writing (though who is to say which is the right way round?) had a peculiar fascination. They were often regarded as magical, containing hidden clues to secret lore. But the link with the Bible was recognized—if only for the sake of confuting and, if possible, converting Jews. When the teaching Order of the Dominicans was founded in the early Thirteenth

[1] Cecil Roth in *Cambridge Medieval History*, vol. vii, p. 651.
[2] See *The Legacy of Israel* (Oxford, 1928), p. 292.

Century, with the express object of saving the world from heresy, its members were called to intensive study of the Bible, and even of such languages as Arabic and Hebrew. It was not long, however, before they secured the right to examine and censor Hebrew books: in the period of the Renaissance they became opponents of Reuchlin, the founder of modern Hebrew studies.

It is pleasing to learn that in the Thirteenth Century, at Ramsey Abbey in the English fens, the Benedictine monks possessed the whole Old Testament in Hebrew. This they obtained by buying up the libraries of the synagogues which had been suppressed at Huntingdon and Stamford. (One wonders how much they paid. In the Fourteenth Century a Bible might cost a priest's whole yearly income.[1]) One of them, Gregory of Huntingdon, was a student also of Greek. Into the monastic library there came Hebrew commentaries, a Hebrew Grammar and Phrase-book, a Greek Grammar and two Greek Psalters. Enough had soon been accumulated to enable a member of the house, Laurence Holbeach, to compile a Hebrew Lexicon.

In Spain Hebrew studies went even further. The whole Old Testament was translated into Castilian in the Fourteenth and Fifteenth Centuries. One of these translations has had a remarkable subsequent history. At the end of the Fifteenth Century Jews were expelled from Spain. They went to the Eastern Mediterranean, taking with them the Spanish language—which is still spoken by Jews in Salonica, Constantinople, Smyrna and elsewhere. They needed a Bible, which was printed for them in Ferrara in 1553. This was based on the old Castilian, written out in Hebrew characters. Another magnificent version produced in Spain was the *Bible of the House of Alba*. This was completed in 1430: and the splendid manuscript volume still exists. The translation was made by a Jew, Moses Aragal, direct from the Hebrew. In one of its illustrations he is shown presenting his Bible to his lord, Don Luis, in the presence of knights of

[1] G. G. Coulton, *Five Centuries of Religion* (Cambridge, 1936), vol. iii, p. 414.

a military order. In the background other knights are shown giving food and drink and clothing to Jews, visiting their sick and burying their dead. Here was an early demonstration in favour of toleration from an unexpected source.[1]

As early as 1369 the Papal Library at Avignon contained a hundred and twenty Hebrew manuscripts but only half a dozen Greek. As the Renaissance developed in Italy there grew an interest in Hebrew. This was not only for the sake of a study of the Biblical text. Scholars were also attracted by the Hebrew *Cabbala*, a series of books written in the Middle Ages, but then thought to be very much older. Some thought they were as old as Abraham! They were based upon the Hebrew Scriptures but contained much that was legendary and magical. Here, men imagined, there might be found the key to all knowledge. Two Italians stand out particularly for their Hebrew studies. The Florentine scholar and statesman, Gianozzo Manetti, in the Fifteenth Century, became a master of the language. He made a collection of Hebrew manuscripts, which is still preserved at the Vatican. He prepared a new translation of the Psalms from Hebrew sources. His collection of manuscripts was partly occasioned by the offer of a large reward by Pope Nicholas V for the discovery of the original Hebrew text of the Gospel of Matthew. He did not succeed: and there are few scholars to-day who are not convinced that —whatever Hebrew or Aramaic documents may lie behind it—the First Gospel is essentially a Greek document.

The second Italian was the young Pico della Mirandola (1463–1494) whose life, written by his nephew, was later to be translated into English by Sir Thomas More. Pico attempted to reconcile Christianity with Greek philosophy. This could best be done, he thought, through the Cabbala. 'There is no science,' he wrote, 'that can more firmly convince us of the divinity of Christ than magic and Cabbala.' He was an able young man, who had a way of scandalizing people.

---

[1] For this paragraph see *The Legacy of Israel*, pp. 310, 311. The illustration described above is reproduced opp. p. 312.

It would naturally be expected that in the Northern Renaissance there would develop an interest in Hebrew similar to the one we have traced in Greek. Was Erasmus to be the hero of this? He was writing to Colet in 1504 or 1505, 'I began also to dip into Hebrew, but, deterred by the strangeness of the words, I desisted, knowing that one man's life and genius are not enough for too many things at a time.'[1] A decade or so later he seemed less 'deterred by the strangeness of the words' and less oppressed by the brevity of life—at least in inciting others to study, for in the Preface to his Greek New Testament he wrote 'A fair knowledge of the three languages, Latin, Greek and Hebrew, of course, are the first things. Nor let the student turn away in despair at the difficulty of this. If you have a teacher and the wish to learn, then these three languages can be learned almost with less labour than every day is spent over the miserable babble of one mongrel language under ignorant teachers.'[2]

Hebrew studies developed in Italy, partly again because of the exodus from Eastern Europe: it was a Jew from Constantinople who taught Pico his Hebrew. It was a German scholar, however, himself a friend of Erasmus and championed by him, who took them furthest. This was Johann Reuchlin (1455–1522). His Italian friends followed the fashion of the time and Graecized his name into Capnion; but it is as Reuchlin that he is best known. He had studied Greek at Paris: the first Greek manuscripts to which he had had access were, oddly enough, those in the Dominican convent at Basle which Erasmus made the basis of his edition. He visited Italy in 1482 in attendance upon the Count of Wurtemburg at the court of Lorenzo di' Medici in Florence; but it was not until 1492, on a later visit, that Pico della Mirandola persuaded him to take up Hebrew and to explore the Cabbala.

On this quest Reuchlin embarked. But he is more important as the father of modern Hebrew studies. In 1506 he

---

[1] Seebohm, *op. cit.*, p. 103.
[2] *Ibid.*, p. 205.

issued his *De Rudimentis Hebraicis*. This was the first Hebrew grammar published by a Christian: it was grammar and lexicon combined. Wars made it difficult to get hold of Hebrew books from Italy, where alone they had been printed so far. He therefore arranged for the publication in Germany of a number of Psalms, with grammatical notes. This was issued in 1512. And all the time, like Erasmus, to whom he comes only second as scholar, he was reading, writing, lecturing and teaching.

These activities were not everywhere approved. In 1509 an enthusiastic convert from Judaism, Johann Pfeffercorn, sought to obtain from the Emperor Maximilian an injunction to suppress all Hebrew books except the Bible. The Emperor consulted Reuchlin, who was naturally opposed to a measure which would remove the very means of his researches. Fortunately the suggestion was dropped. The Dominicans next accused Reuchlin of heresy. His case was tried. He was acquitted by the Bishop of Speyer, acting on the Pope's behalf, who confirmed his action. His victory gave a great fillip to Greek and Hebrew studies.

Meanwhile the Hebrew Bible was being put into print. Christians divide their Bible into two main sections, the Old and the New Testaments, or, more properly, the Holy Scriptures of the Old Covenant and the Holy Scriptures of the New Covenant. The Jews divide their Scriptures— our Old Testament—into three. First—and first also in importance—is the *Law*; the first five books of the Bible, in which there is set out the way of life of a people under obedience to God. The second great section is that of the *Prophets*. This is divided into the Earlier Prophets, which contain what we would call the historical books of Joshua, Judges, Samuel and Kings—history written from God's point of view. The Later Prophets were usually made up of four rolls: one contained Isaiah, another Jeremiah, another Ezekiel, and the fourth 'the book of the Twelve', what we normally, and somewhat erroneously—following a Latin title—call the Minor Prophets. (There was nothing 'minor'

about Amos or Hosea!) Daniel had no place in the pro-
phetic books, nor had the Books of Chronicles. These, along
with Psalms, Proverbs, Job and a number of others, composed the miscellaneous section of the *Writings* or Hagio-
grapha.

It was natural that the considerable task of printing the
Hebrew Bible should follow this order and that it should be
carried out in Italy. Actually, however, the first book of the
Hebrew Scriptures to appear in print was the Psalter, with
a commentary, printed in 1477, probably at Bologna. The
Law (or Pentateuch) was printed there first in 1482, the
Prophets came in two volumes from Soncino in 1485 and the
Writings from Naples in 1487. Thus Jewish enterprise had
printed the whole Old Testament in Hebrew nearly thirty
years before Christian enterprise had issued the much
smaller New Testament in Greek. (The Latin Bible, we
have already seen, was the first book to be printed in
Europe, in 1456.) Soncino was the name of a Jewish family
of printers, derived from the small town of Soncino near
Milan. Their enterprise even occasioned a parody of
Isaiah 2.3. 'Out of Zion shall go forth the Law, and the
word of the Lord from Soncino.' Official Rabbinic Bibles
followed. The first, issued in four volumes from Venice in
1516 and 1517, introduced into the Hebrew Bible the
Christian chapter divisions. These derived originally from
Stephen Langton, Archbishop of Canterbury at the time
of the signing of Magna Carta in 1215, who had inserted
them into the Latin Bible ten years earlier.

Meanwhile there was being issued at Alcala the Complutensian Polyglot. Among the scholars who worked for
Cardinal Ximenes were three converts from Judaism. In
this great edition the Hebrew, Greek and Latin texts were
set out side by side. It was the Hebrew text of the Complutensian Polyglot that Tyndale used in his translations of the
Old Testament: it had thus considerable influence in
determining our Authorised Version. To the Hebrew text
there was added in the Polyglot the *Targum* of Onkelos.

This was an early rendering—in part translation, in part paraphrase—of the Hebrew Scriptures into Aramaic. The purpose of these Targums, of which there were several, was to enable a reader with little Hebrew to understand the meaning of the Scriptures in his own language. It will readily be understood that they have great importance for the Biblical student.

As modern scholarship developed two rather surprising facts became clear. The first was that the manuscripts of the Hebrew Old Testament which scholars had to work upon were neither as ancient as many of the New nor even as some of the translation into Greek of the same Hebrew Scriptures. The second was that a far greater similarity existed between Hebrew manuscripts of the Old Testament than between Greek manuscripts of the New. Indeed it was long believed that the variations were so few that all must go back to one original manuscript or archetype: and though this theory has been discarded by the most recent scholarship, and though new discoveries of manuscripts have been made and greater varieties discerned within those already studied the essential similarity of text remains. What can account for these facts?

In the Revised Version of 1884 the translators of the Old Testament wrote in the Preface that, in the matter of text, 'the task of the Revisers has been much simpler than that which the New Testament Company had before them. The Received, or, as it is commonly called, the Massoretic Text of the Old Testament Scriptures has come down to us in manuscripts which are of no very great antiquity, and which all belong to the same family or recension.' The word *Massoretic* refers to a body of Jewish scholars called the Massoretes (from *Massôrâ*, tradition) whose work culminated in the Tenth Century A.D. Their work was essentially conservative. Their aim was the exact preservation of the text as it had come down to them; and if in one place a letter was elongated or enlarged they were careful to copy it out exactly as it was written. They went in

for minute calculations which to the modern mind might
appear ludicrous or, at the least, pedantic—numbering the
letters in a book, for example, and discovering the middle
letter—but which had nevertheless the admirable effect of
preserving the text as they had inherited it. Modern scholars
have reason to be grateful that the Massoretes would not
have agreed with Saint Paul that 'the letter killeth'.

The Massoretes found, of course, variations in the manuscripts upon which they worked, and what were clearly
mistakes. This did not lead them to make alterations to the
text itself—it was too precious to be tampered with—but
to make notes in the margin of what was to be read (*Keri*)
in place of what was actually written (*Kethibh*). Modern
translators have often to decide which they are to
prefer, the text or the margin. The Revised Version translators have preferred the text most often, but not always;
and an indication of the *Keri* is often given in their margin
as an alternative reading.

The work of the Massoretes was necessary from the very
nature of the Hebrew language and from the fact that it
was no longer a spoken language in daily life. The written
Hebrew consists only of consonants—in this it is like modern
shorthand. A shorthand writer has little difficulty in sup-
plying the necessary vowels from a recollection of the spoken
word: with somebody else's script, or with a script some
years old it would be more difficult and mistakes might
be difficult to avoid. In Hebrew the consonants DBR—
which would be written דבר from right to left—might mean
speak or *speaking* or *he spoke* or *word* or *pestilence*. The meaning
could usually be understood from the context. But not
always. Doubt might arise. Why not insert vowels into the
text? This was debarred because the text was too holy to
be interfered with. Various expedients were tried until the
Massoretes invented a series of 'vowel points', little signs
which were inserted around the letters—not interfering
with any of them—to indicate what vowels were to be read.
(It is to be remembered that until quite modern times

reading almost always meant reading aloud.) Thus דֹּבֵר,
dobhèr means *speaking*: דִּבֶּר *dibber* means *to speak*: דֶּבֶר *debher*
means *pestilence* and דָּבָר *dabhar* means *word*. The actual
letters have not been altered at all: the 'pointing' has
added the vowels while the central dot has hardened the
d and doubled the b. This complicated but ingenious
system existed in more than one form. That which was
developed in Tiberias by the Tenth Century became
standardised and is to be found in printed Hebrew Bibles
to-day.

Very great care was always taken in copying. It was
insisted that every page should be according to an approved
pattern, down to the number of lines on a page and the
exact formation of the letters. If a copy of the Law had two
errors on a page it might be corrected: if there were three
it had to be discarded. A purist might maintain that a
scroll with one error on a page was invalid. This is a description of how the work was done, according to the rules
laid down in the Talmud, the Jewish traditional law:

A synagogue roll must be written on the skin of clean
animals, prepared for the particular use of the synagogue
by a Jew. These must be fastened together with strings
taken from clean animals. Every skin must contain an
equal number of columns, equal throughout the entire
codex. The length of each column must not extend over
less than forty-eight, or more than sixty lines; and the
breadth must consist of thirty letters. The whole copy
must be first lined; and if three words be written in it
without a line it is worthless. The ink should be black,
neither red, green, nor any other colour, and be prepared
according to a definite receipt. An *authentic* copy must be
the exemplar, from which the transcriber ought not in
the least to deviate. No word or letter, not even a *yod*,
must be written from memory, the scribe not having
looked at the codex before him ... Between every consonant
the space of a hair or thread must intervene; between

every new *parshiah*, or section, the breadth of nine consonants; between every book, three lines. The fifth book
of Moses must terminate exactly with a line; but the rest
need not do so. Besides this, the copyist must sit in full
Jewish dress, wash his whole body, not begin to write the
name of God with a pen newly dipped in ink, and should
a king address him while writing that name he must take
no notice of him . . . The rolls in which these regulations
are not observed are condemned to be buried in the
ground or burned; or they are banished to the schools,
to be used as reading-books.[1]

To the Jewish rabbis, or teachers, every bit of vellum or
papyrus on which Scripture had been written was important because it might contain the holy name of God.
Yet old books did not possess for them the antiquarian value
which they have for modern scholars. What was needed was a
copy that was accurate and that was clean. When sacred
books were worn out they were put on one side. There was a
special chamber adjoining the synagogue called the Geniza
where these worn out books were put. (In many English
church vestries or lumber-rooms there will be found old desk
Prayer Books, dating from Victorian or earlier times, which
no one quite knows what to do with.) From time to time the
Geniza would be cleared out and its contents buried.
Sometimes a worn-out roll of the Law would be buried
by the side of a scholar.

This meticulous care in copying ensured that the Massoretic text, as it emerged in the Tenth Century of our era,
was substantially what it was in the First and that it was
hardly corrupted at all in the centuries that followed. It
was, indeed, in the early years of the Christian era that a
new emphasis was placed by the Jews upon the importance
of their Scriptures. Their Temple was destroyed in the fall
of Jerusalem in A.D. 70: now they had only their Bibles
left—and these also were in imminent danger of destruction.

---

[1] Davidson, *Introduction to the Old Testament*, 1856, p. 89, quoted Kenyon,
Our Bible and the Ancient Manuscripts, p. 39.

More than ever Judaism became the religion of a book. A great Jewish scholar of modern times, the late Dr. C. G. Montefiore has called this destruction of the Temple with the consequent end of animal sacrifices 'the crowning mercy in the history of Judaism . . . Rabbi was an immense improvement upon Priest.'[1] And the Rabbis guarded the text of the Scriptures more jealously than ever before.

Until recently it would be said that we had no certain knowledge of manuscripts of the Massoretic text earlier than the end of the Ninth Century A.D. It is likely that the fullest and most authoritative of these is one in a synagogue at Aleppo: but this is unfortunately not available for Western scholars to publish or use. Its owners will not allow it to pass from their hands nor to be photographed or published; though Rabbis may consult it for verification and reference. Other early manuscripts are in Leningrad and Oxford and Cambridge.

Two questions may well arise from this chapter. Were the contents of a Geniza ever discovered in modern times? The answer is Yes. The contents of the Geniza of the Synagogue of Old Cairo, now treasured possessions of many libraries, have thrown great light upon Biblical studies. Has it been possible to discover a Hebrew text from earlier than Massoretic times? The finding of what are called the Dead Sea Scrolls—which include a complete manuscript of Isaiah—have given scholars Biblical documents to work on hundreds of years older than anything they had before in Hebrew. There are some who believe that these documents date from before the time of Christ. These are matters which must be considered in a later chapter.

[1] *Record and Revelation* (edited H. Wheeler Robinson), Oxford, 1938, p. 439.

Chapter Four

THE DOMINANCE OF LATIN

IN HIS study of *Church Life in England in the Thirteenth Century*,[1] Dr. J. R. H. Moorman writes of the knowledge of the Bible possessed by the laity at that time: 'Their ideas were no doubt often muddled, and much of their knowledge of the Bible was confused with apocryphal and legendary stories, but it is questionable whether the average peasant or artisan of the thirteenth century was actually any less familiar with the Bible narratives than his descendant of the present day.' This does not indicate an exalted view of the Thirteenth Century so much as a depressed view of the Twentieth. In a footnote we are told that this statement 'rests upon two suppositions; one that knowledge of Bible stories was more general in the thirteenth century than is sometimes imagined; the other that knowledge of the Bible is extremely limited at the present day. Only an historian can test the first, and only some one who has worked for some time as a parish priest can test the second. The experience of those who have worked in parishes in recent years is that a great many people have only the very slightest acquaintance with the Bible, while a generation is growing up containing a certain number who are ignorant of even the most familiar passages.'

The great difference, of course, is in the widespread availability of the Bible to-day and the widespread ability to read. Yet it is proverbial that a horse may be led to the water without being made to drink. Superabundance of supply can produce a restriction of demand; and there may be some to-day who would like to return to that earlier time when, in John Foxe's words, 'some gave five

---

[1] Cambridge, 1946, p. 102.

marks,[1] some more, some less, for a book: some gave a load of hay for a few chapters of St. James, or of St. Paul in English ... To see their travails, their earnest seekings, their burning zeal, their readings, their watchings, their sweet assemblies, their love and concord, their godly living, their faithful demeaning with the faithful, may make us now, in these our days of free profession, to blush for shame.'

Every generation can find something in the life of an earlier one to shame it. Foxe wrote at a time when the Bible was at last available in English and no longer forbidden literature, widely read at last through its being printed and because a greater number of people were being taught to read. In the Middle Ages the situation was different. In the Fourteenth Century people would give a great deal for a fragment of the Bible in English because they had not seen it in English before. The Bible possessed not only an imperious claim as God's word but the powerful attraction of novelty. When English Bibles were first set up in churches; and when people first owned copies of their own they proved as powerful magnets as wireless sets in the first days of broadcasting. William Malden, for example, recalled later that 'immediately dyveres poore men in the towne of Chelmysford in the county of Essex, where my father dwelled and I borne and with him brought up, the sayd poore men bought the Newe Testament of Jesus Christ and on Sundays did sit redinge in the lower end of the church and many would floke about them to heare theyr redinge.'[2] In 1881, when the Revised Version of the New Testament was first published, an observer in the City of London noted people reading it in the streets as they came from the shops. But the practice did not persist.

[1] In Dr. John Brown's *History of the English Bible*, a Cambridge Manual published in 1911, from which this quotation is borrowed, the words are here inserted in brackets 'equal to about £40 in our money.' The reader can work out for himself what the sum is worth now! In 1222 the Council of Oxford laid down that the stipends of vicars ought to be at least five marks a year, except in Wales, 'where vicars are content with less by reason of the poverty of their churches.' (Margaret Deanesly, *The Significance of the Latin Bible*, London, 1951, p. 6).

[2] Quoted from Strype's *Memorials of Cranmer* by John William Adamson, *The Illiterate Anglo-Saxon* (Cambridge, 1946), p. 44.

To-day many people own Bibles which they never read. In the Middle Ages most people knew stories from a Bible which they had scarcely seen and could not read. There are three things especially which must be realised about the Bible in the Middle Ages.

First, copies of the Bible had to be made by hand. They were therefore rare, cumbrous and expensive.

Second, the priests themselves were rarely well-trained in biblical knowledge: what most of them could hand on to their people was limited and confused with non-biblical material.

Third, the Bible was in Latin, and its translation into other languages, except for the use of royalty and high nobility, was forbidden.

These facts must be examined.

Bible-readers, who nowadays are accustomed to the possession of small, portable editions, seldom reflect upon how great a triumph of the printer's and the paper-maker's skill lies behind the production of these volumes in large quantities at low cost. Far more often they complain about the printing of the Bible, with no knowledge of the technical problems which have to be overcome for the setting out of so great a mass of literature between the covers of one book. If they want larger type, more ample margins and better spacing, the book must inevitably be much larger. An illustration of this is the beautifully produced *Bible Designed to be Read as Literature*, which is a large volume at a price beyond the reach of those who buy Bibles in quantities. Nor is it complete. To the Middle Ages, however, it would have seemed a comparatively small book, its pages a miracle of thinness. The Latin Bible of the Middle Ages could not be set out in one volume. It needed at least two large folio volumes—often as many as four. Written script, even when the words are partially contracted by a sort of shorthand, takes up much more space than modern printing. The vellum on which the script was set out—often with much beauty—was also far thicker than modern paper.

All hand-produced books were expensive. It was not unknown in the Thirteenth Century for a man to take legal action to secure the return of a book which had been borrowed.[1] When a Thirteenth Century Bishop of Hereford died he directed that his larger Bible be sold in order to provide clothes for the poor.[2] A contemporary Bishop of Winchester, though he possessed other books, had no Bible at all, but had to borrow one from the local Convent.[3] The cost of a Bible in the Fourteenth Century, wrote Coulton, might easily amount to a priest's whole yearly income.[4] The ordinary priest rarely handled a volume of the Bible itself. But he knew the parts which came in services. He probably knew the Psalms better than he knew the New Testament. In the monasteries, 'the religious man's inner life was above all in the Psalter . . . The very sound of the chant became part of a man's life, bench answering manfully to bench, while their breath rose in the frosty air of a midnight choir.'[5]

When the Reformation came in England one of the chief aims of the reformers was to restore the custom of the ancient Fathers, who 'so ordered the matter, that all the whole Bible (or the greatest part thereof) should be read over once every year . . . But these many years passed, this godly and decent order of the ancient Fathers hath been so altered, broken, and neglected, by planting in uncertain stories, and legends, with multitude of responds, verses, vain repetitions, commemorations, and synodals; that commonly when any book of the Bible was begun, after three or four chapters were read out, all the rest were left unread. And in this sort the book of Isaiah was begun in Advent, and the book of Genesis in Septuagesima; but they were only begun, and never read through: after like sort were other books of Holy Scripture used.'[6]

[1] Moorman, op. cit., p. 157n. [2] Ibid., p. 182. [3] Ibid., p. 181.
[4] Five Centuries of Religion (Cambridge, 1936), vol. iii, p. 414.
[5] Ibid., vol i, p. 96.
[6] Of Ceremonies. Why Some be Abolished, and Some Retained, which follows the Preface in the Book of Common Prayer, but was Cranmer's Preface to the Prayer Book of 1549.

There were, of course, men of the Middle Ages who knew the Bible very well indeed. Supreme among these was St. Bernard (1090–1153), of whom Dr. Coulton wrote that he 'knew his Bible inside and out; Luther and Bunyan knew it no better . . . The Bible became bone of his bone and flesh of his flesh. Thus men noted that, when he spoke from the Bible, it was as if he were composing, and not repeating; as if the Holy Ghost were speaking directly from his mouth.'[1] With ordinary men the situation was different. To quote Dr. Coulton again, 'The rough truth may be put very simply; the best medieval writers knew their Vulgate very well; a great many knew parts of it well enough, especially those portions which happened to come in their service-books. The average priest knew nothing outside those service-books, and not even all that was inside; the lower priesthood, as Roger Bacon and other equally credible witnesses testify, understood little or nothing even of their church offices. The laity could seldom read Latin with any ease, beyond the sort of hotel-waiter's vocabulary with which a few men wrote their accounts or a scrivener his legal formulae; therefore the most educated and ambitious seldom got far beyond the Psalms and the Sunday Gospels and Epistles. A few of the richest possessed Bibles in French or Psalters in French or English; but, as soon as a general desire for vernacular translation arose, this was opposed by the ecclesiastical authorities, and for the rest of the Middle Ages vernacular Bibles were either explicitly condemned, or lay under a strong suspicion of heresy.'[2]

The Bible was large and expensive and hard to come by; though by the end of the Middle Ages it had become commoner and cheaper. Only a small minority of the clergy were really familiar with it. And it was in Latin. As Cranmer complained, 'whereas St. Paul would have such language spoken to the people in the Church, as they might understand, and have profit by hearing the same; the

[1] *Op. cit.*, vol. i, p. 291 ff.
[2] *Ibid.*

Service in this Church of England these many years hath been read in Latin to the people, which they understand not; so that they have heard with their ears only, and their heart, spirit, and mind, have not been edified thereby.'[1]

Most modern Christians would agree with Cranmer: to them the prohibition of vernacular translations appears obscurantist and wrong. To the vast majority of medieval Christians it appeared natural and right. When it was questioned, as it came to be, its defence was based upon the distinction drawn in the Epistle to the Hebrews between milk and solid meat. A Fourteenth Century writer in the Low Countries interpreted this distinction. There were, he said, the simple and open doctrines and those which were deep and obscure. The first he defined as 'such as the lives and deeds of the saints, the passions and triumphs of the martyrs, and other teaching concerning vices and virtues, the glory of the saints and the miseries of the damned, and books like these which are plain and open.'[2] This list, upon examination, might be found to contain hardly any Scriptural material at all.

In the Middle Ages the ordained were enjoined to read the Scriptures but not the laity. These were to hear and accept what their teachers found in them, but not themselves to go to the source direct. 'When the Waldensian and Lollard heretics complained that the laity were ignorant of the Scriptures since they could not read Latin and were not allowed to read translations, the orthodox answer was always, that it was the duty of the laity to listen to the Scriptures, as expounded verbally by the priest, in accordance with the holy doctors.'[3] This might suggest that at the Mass the Epistle and Gospel were translated for the groundlings by the priest; but there is little evidence for this until the very eve of the Reformation.[4] If the Church claimed to be giving its untutored children milk rather than meat it was

---

[1] *Of Ceremonies.*
[2] *The Lollard Bible*, by Margaret Deanesly (Cambridge, 1920), p. 96.
[3] *Ibid.*, p. 197.
[4] *Ibid.*, p. 199.

seldom the wholly pure milk of the Gospel. In the Middle Ages, as to-day, books of ready-made sermons were available for the clergy. Those in one notable collection 'deal with the virtues and vices of all classes of society, monks, priests and seculars: but no single story can be found to advocate the practice of reading the Bible, either by clerks or lay people.'[1]

The idea crystallized in medieval practice was that there were two kinds of Christians, those who were 'in the know' and those who were not. The distinction could be defended from Scripture: 'Unto you is given the mystery of the kingdom of God: but unto them that are without, all things are done in parables.'[2] Who were they to cast pearls before swine or give that which is holy unto dogs? *Nolite sanctum dare canibus*—the words resounded like the response to a versicle whenever the translation of the Scriptures was mooted. Nor was this line taken only by inquisitors and by men who were notably narrow-minded. No man of the Thirteenth Century was more anxious than Bishop Grossteste of Lincoln to spread scriptural knowledge; yet he never advocated the translation of the Scriptures into English.[3] In Italy, in the Fifteenth Century, the Dominican reformer, Savonarola, who laid great stress on biblical knowledge, encouraging the study of the learned languages as an aid to biblical interpretation, never went so far as to advocate translation into Italian.[4] Earlier in the same century, Jean Gerson, Chancellor of the University of Paris and the greatest scholar of the day, was also the chief advocate of papal reform. In theology he was something of a modernist, breaking away from the stranglehold of the scholastic system. Yet the very scheme of Church reform which he presented to the Council of Constance included a formal condemnation of vernacular translation: 'Now this use of holy scripture by modern men as if holy scripture should be believed in its bare text without the help of any interpretation

[1] *Ibid.*, p. 201.
[2] Mk. 3.11.
[3] Deanesly, *op. cit.*, p. 182.
[4] *Ibid.*, p. 47.

or explanation, is a kind of use which is attended by
grave dangers and scandals . . . Moreover the errors of the
Beghards and the Poor Men of Lyons and the like have
sprung from this pestiferous root, and do daily increase:
because there are many lay people who have a translation
of the Bible into the vulgar tongue, to the great prejudice and
scandal of catholic truth, and it is proposed in this scheme
of reform that this should be abolished.'[1]

Not only was the Bible in Latin, occluded from popular
use. Those who studied it most came to doubt whether
they had before them a really accurate text: indeed they
became sure that it was corrupt. This certainty was expressed, in particular, by the Thirteenth Century Franciscan,
Roger Bacon. He complained also that the Church in the
West was cut off from the experience and tradition of the
Church in the East. Why were not the Greek Fathers being
translated into Latin? And why did not the Pope do some-
thing about it? 'Numberless books, again, of Hebrew and
Greek expositors are wanting to the Latins: as those of
Origen, Basil, Gregory Nazianzen, Damascene, Dionysius,
Chrysostom, and other most notable Doctors, alike in
Hebrew and in Greek. The Church, therefore, is slumbering.
She does nothing in this matter, nor hath done these seventy
years: save that my Lord Robert [Grosseteste] Bishop of
Lincoln, of holy memory, did give to the Latins some part
of the writings of St. Dionysius and of Damascene, and some
other holy Doctors. It is an amazing thing, this negligence
of the Church: for, from the time of Pope Damasus there
hath not been any Pope, nor any of less rank, who hath
busied himself for the advantaging of the Church by translations, except the aforesaid glorious Bishop.'[2]

For the ordinary medieval scholar the Latin Bible was
the starting-point. He had no thought of Hebrew or Greek
further back. The text was there, for him to interpret along
certain   well-defined   lines: there   was   the   allegorical

---

[1] *Ibid.*, p. 103.
[2] Quoted, M. R. James, in *The Cambridge Modern History*, vol. i, p. 585.

interpretation, which was a favourite and provided an easy way of removing difficulties, the tropological or historical, and the anagogical or mystical. When Roger Bacon emphasised the importance of the literal interpretation a new day was dawning. And directly the literal interpretation became important a new importance was attached to the accuracy of the text. A later Franciscan than Bacon, Nicholas de Lyra—who died in 1340—complained that 'the literal sense is much obscured through the manner of exposition handed down from others.' For him the literal sense was the foundation; but it was obscured 'partly through the fault of scribes, who through the similarity of letters have in many places written otherwise than the true text has it; partly through the influence of certain correctors, who have in many places inserted vowel points where they should not be, and begun or ended verses where they ought not to begin or end.'[1] This scientific interest in the text and what lay behind it was a sign of the coming Renaissance.

How did the Bible come to be in Latin at all? None of it was written in that language. The New Testament emerged within the Roman Empire, but within that Eastern section of it which had Greek, and not Latin, for its second language, dominant, for purposes of culture and commerce over all forms of local speech. The book with which the first Christian missionaries went out was not the Hebrew Old Testament— nor yet the New Testament, for it had not been written. It was the Greek version of the Old Testament, usually known as the *Septuagint*. St. Mark's Gospel is thought to have been written in Rome for the Church there: it certainly contains some 'Latinisms'—but it was written in Greek. So was St. Paul's Epistle to the Romans. The first Church in Rome must have been predominantly Greek-speaking, largely composed of recent immigrants to the city. When Tacitus made a reference to Christianity in his account of the fire of Rome in A.D. 64, he expressed surprise that the pernicious superstition had broken out again, not only in

[1] Deanesly, *op. cit.*, p. 166.

Judaea, where the mischief had originated, but in Rome itself. Yet was not that city 'the receptacle for everything that is sordid and degraded from every quarter of the globe'? The satirical poet Juvenal complained that the Syrian river Orontes had flowed into the Roman Tiber. The Christian Church in Rome must have appeared very like a foreign congregation in Soho to-day. The influence of Christians grew; but they still clung to the Greek language and the Greek Bible. The official Empire used two languages; the Church only one.

Change was inevitable, from the very necessities of the missionary situation. There came a time when, as Augustine later complained, 'whoever chanced upon a Greek codex and thought he had a little aptitude in both Latin and Greek attempted a translation.'[1] Unfortunately there was not among these Latin translators and copyists any of the discipline which, as we have seen, guided the Jewish scribe as he made every line of every letter. With translation and copying there came a corruption of the text. In time, however, there emerged what is known as the Old Latin version of the Bible—though whether it is right to speak of one Old Latin version or of a plurality of such versions scholars are not agreed. It was a translation into Latin of the Greek Bible: so far as the Old Testament was concerned it was a translation of a translation. Yet it is possible that behind parts of the Old Testament there may lie a rudimentary translation into Latin made for Roman and North African Jews even before Christian times. Certainly there must have been a considerable amount of oral translation in synagogue worship: the existence of a written translation has been inferred.[2]

The Old Latin does not exist to-day in any complete form. Much of the Old Testament is missing; though a good deal can be pieced together from quotations in the Latin Fathers. For the New Testament there are a good many

[1] Quoted, H. F. D. Sparks, in *The Bible in Its English & Ancient Versions*, edited by H. Wheeler Robinson (Oxford, 1940), p. 103.
[2] See Sparks, *op. cit.*, p. 102.

manuscripts. The late date of some of them indicates that the Old Latin was still being copied long after it had passed out of official favour. A Gospel codex at Vercelli in North Italy—known as *a*—is almost certainly the oldest. It is believed to have been written by the hand of Bishop Euse-bius, who was martyred in 371. It has been treated as a sacred relic, and so affected by the kisses of worshippers throughout many centuries that it has had to be repaired.

An authoritative revision of the Latin Bible was needed. In 382 Pope Damasus commissioned his secretary, whom we know as Jerome, to prepare this. Jerome was the greatest scholar of the day, and had recently returned from a visit to the East. People made a lot of him in Rome: his *Letters from the Desert* were everywhere being quoted. They had made asceticism exciting. Many thought that he would be the next Pope. Now he went quickly to work; and in 383 he produced his version of the Four Gospels. The book was prefaced with a dedication to Pope Damasus, in which he explained the circumstances of its preparation. He had been asked to revise the Latin according to 'the true Greek text'—and he was himself to decide what that true text was. He knew that his work would provoke opposition—was there ever a translation of the Scriptures which did not?— and he was as conservative in making alterations as his scholarship would allow him to be. In many ways his work was a revision rather than a new translation. After pro-ducing a first version of the Psalms, he went on with the rest of the New Testament. But it is uncertain how much of this is actually his work. In his commentaries on the Epistles Jerome quotes the Scriptures from a text much nearer to the Old Latin than it is to 'Jerome's Vulgate'—as if he were ignorant of his own work.

At the end of 384 Pope Damasus died—and Jerome was not chosen to succeed him. He left for the Holy Land, determined to spend the rest of his life in biblical learning supported by spiritual asceticism. He established himself in Bethlehem in monastic state, with members of a convent

recruited from the daughters of society ladies in Rome, near
by, unobtrusively fetching and carrying. 'In this little villa
of Christ,' wrote Jerome, 'everything is rustic, and apart
from the singing of psalms there is silence. As the ploughman
drives his share, he sings his *alleluia*. The sweating reaper
diverts himself with psalms, and the vine-dresser as he clips
the shoots with his reaping-knife hums the songs of David.
These are the only songs sung here. These are our popular
love-songs. They are the songs sung by the shepherds, who
come to hearten the tillers of the soil.'[1] Here Jerome remained
for the last thirty-four years of his life, conducting an
enormous correspondence and receiving the visits of friends,
writing many books and—in the intervals—translating
the Old Testament.

Jerome's work on the Old Testament was much more
revolutionary than on the New; more upsetting to the con-
servatives; more resented by his opponents. He learned
Hebrew so as to go back to the originals. He complained
that it was a very difficult task, but very rewarding. He
never became a very proficient Hebrew scholar; and for
the translation of certain books he was specially coached
by a rabbi: but the very fact of going to the Hebrew at all
was resented. Was he not going over to the Jews, by accepting
their Bible in place of the Greek Bible upon which the
whole Christian Church had been brought up? Even
Augustine 'believed in the "divine inspiration" of the
Greek Old Testament, and he frequently stated that it
was of a higher spiritual value than the Hebrew Bible.'[2]

Modern scholars have reason to be thankful that Jerome
thought differently from Augustine. Jerome was at work
on the Hebrew Bible hundreds of years before the production of the earliest Hebrew manuscripts which we
possess, apart from the recently discovered Dead Sea
Scrolls. He was at work before the revision of the text by

---

[1] *Epistolae*, LXXVII, 7. Quoted Robert Payne, *The Fathers of the Western Church* (London, 1952), p. 89.
[2] Bleddyn J. Roberts, *The Old Testament Text and Versions* (Cardiff, University of Wales Press, 1951), p. 250.

the Massoretes. The Latin Bible which he prepared is therefore an independent authority for the nature of the early Hebrew text.

We have seen that in the Fifteenth Century Jean Gerson complained that many people had a translation of the Bible into the vulgar tongue, to the great prejudice and scandal of catholic truth. But the Latin Bible, whose pre-eminent authority he was endeavouring to safeguard, was, in its origin, a translation 'into the vulgar tongue', the speech of the people rather than literary Latin.

The Greek Old Testament was a larger book than the Scriptures accepted as canonical in Hebrew. It was, indeed, the Bible of the Dispersion: its Daniel was much longer than the Hebrew one: and there are other books which— along with the additional chapters of Daniel—are nowadays usually called the Apocrypha. These passed into the Latin Bible; and in the Middle Ages many people were more familiar with some of the incidents they contained than with much in the Gospels themselves. For the Church of England these books are regarded as of subordinate im- portance: and the Sixth of the Thirty-nine Articles in the Prayer Book quotes the opinion of Jerome that the Church doth read them 'for example of life and instruction of manners; but yet doth it not apply them to establish any doctrine.' Jerome did not think much of these books; and he did not spend much time on them. Two of them were in Aramaic, Tobit and Judith. He spent a day over the first and a night over the second, getting a Jew to translate them into Hebrew, while he dictated them to a secretary in Latin. The 'ecclesiastical books', Wisdom, Ecclesiasticus, 1 and 2 Maccabees and Baruch he left as he had found them in the Old Latin: and so they remain in the Vulgate to-day.[1]

Gradually the Vulgate supplanted the Old Latin; though this was still being used by Aelfric and Dunstan in England in the Tenth Century. It was not until the Council of Trent in 1546 that the Vulgate became the standard for the Roman

[1] Roberts, *op. cit.*, p. 253.

Catholic Church as a whole. By the middle of the Sixth Century the text of the Vulgate, like its Old Latin predecessor, was showing signs of becoming corrupt: the errors and interpretations of copyists were having their effect. Alcuin of York produced a revision for the Emperor Charlemagne at the end of the Eighth Century. Lanfranc, who was Archbishop of Canterbury in the time of William the Conqueror, prepared another and Stephen Harding issued another for the monks of the Cistercian Order. In the Thirteenth Century an authoritative version was made by the University of Paris. Nevertheless, Roger Bacon called upon the Pope to prepare an official edition, and in the days of the Renaissance Erasmus made the same demand. Much work has been done on the Vulgate in modern times, and in recent years the monks of the Benedictine Order have been at work upon a new and authoritative version. The Vulgate is also the basis of a notable modern translation of the Bible into English 'for private use only' by Monsignor Ronald Knox. He translates from the Latin; but is always aware of the Greek and Hebrew versions, to which he makes frequent reference in footnotes.

Some of the earliest manuscripts of the Vulgate are connected with England. There is a complete manuscript of the New Testament—with the Gospels arranged as one continuous story, in a form originated by Tatian in the second century, called the *Diatessaron*—which was written about 545 for Victor, the Bishop of Capua. This was brought to Jarrow, probably by Benedict Biscop, around 681. Later it was given to Boniface, the missionary of Germany, who gave it to his monastery at Fulda, where it still is. It is known as *Codex Fuldensis*. One of the greatest of all manuscripts of the Vulgate is known as *Codex Amiatinus*, which was written at Jarrow before 715 for presentation to the Pope. It was formerly in the monastery of Monte Amiata, but is now the greatest treasure of the Laurentian Library in Florence. The famous Lindisfarne Gospels in the British Museum were written by Eadfrith, Bishop of Lindisfarne from 698 to 721, in honour of his predecessor, St. Cuthbert, who died in 687. This we learn from a colophon—an ornamental tail-piece to a book, giving information which is nowadays put on the title-page—written in the Tenth Century by a priest named Aldred. He told how Eadfrith wrote the book; how his successor, Æthelwald, pressed and bound it, and that an anchorite, or recluse, named Billfrith, ornamented its binding with metal-work and gems. Aldred himself glossed the book —that is to say, provided it with a translation between the lines—into the Northumbrian dialect. The volume is one of great beauty, being decorated with patterns of surprising intricacy.

Jerome's translation of the Old Testament was from the Hebrew. But before he translated the Psalter from the Hebrew he made two versions of it from the Greek. The second, known as the Gallican Psalter, passed into the Vulgate. Coverdale's translation of the Bible into English was from the Vulgate. It was his translation of the Psalms which—by way of the Great Bible of 1539—was adopted as the Psalter in the Book of Common Prayer. An Anglican congregation singing the Psalms is thus using the work of Jerome; based, indeed, upon that of Origen about a hundred and fifty years earlier. But that is another story, to which we shall return in a later chapter.

Chapter Five

BACK TO THE MISSIONARIES – I

THE FACT that vernacular translations of the Scriptures were so sternly forbidden in the later Middle Ages and those who owned them so rigorously prosecuted is a clear indication that there was a growing popular demand for the Scriptures in language which common people could understand. Ecclesiastical authorities were intolerant of this demand and frightened by it because it was usually associated with what they regarded as a revolutionary desire to overhaul the organization of the Church and to simplify its doctrine. Against such proposals they stood firm, with the rigidity of men in possession. It was one thing for a king to have the Bible in French, or for English nuns to read the Psalms in English under the direction of their confessor; but it was quite another thing when 'the very cooks who sod the pottage made good their claim to read the Bible in Wycliffe's English.'[1]

The translation of the Bible into English was the end rather than the beginning of John Wycliffe's schemes of reform; and the greater part of the work was done by his learned secretary, John Purvey. His movement was, in its origins, scholarly and theological, an Oxford movement: some of the first preaching associated with it was done by young men in the vacations, very much as young men from the Universities and theological colleges are now wont to descend upon English parishes for short missions. As this work developed—and as controversy increased—there came with it an appeal to the Scriptures as 'Goddis Law' over against the man-made laws of the Church. Often the sentiment was repeated that the Gospel is the rule by which all Christians ought to live. Whereas later reformers broke

[1] Henry IV, III, 433, quoted Deanesly, *op. cit.*, p. 294.

through rules to the liberty of the Gospel, Wycliffe and
his Lollard followers found in the Scriptures the true rule
of life.

It was natural that passages of Scripture should be read
at their meetings. It was natural that they should be read
in English. The translation of isolated passages led to the
demand for a complete translation; and this is what Wycliffe's
version of the Bible was, a complete translation of the Vulgate—including the Apocrypha—something quite new in
English history. Because the Scriptures were regarded as a
body of law to replace the Church's law the first of the two
Lollard translations was extremely literal both in wording
and in order. But this 'crib' to the Vulgate—something in
the manner which memory associates with *Kelly's Keys*—
was extremely useful for purposes of argument.

The first translation was carried out, at Wycliffe's instigation, by five Oxford scholars, working under his principal
assistant, Nicholas Hereford. Hereford's own work on the
Old Testament breaks off abruptly in the middle of a verse,
Baruch 3.20—perhaps because of his arrest and trial at
Canterbury, where he was excommunicated. His original
manuscript, with corrections in his own hand, is in the
Bodleian Library at Oxford. The whole Bible, in this
version, was in circulation by Wycliffe's death in 1384—
though more in bits and pieces than in whole volumes.
It is full of constructions like 'Sothli, hem rowynge, he
slepte . . . And he risynge blamyde the winde . . . And the
breed takun, he dide thankingis.' A schoolmaster might
here note the very echoes of the classroom. The version
rendered the ablative absolute as schoolboys do to this
day. Sometimes following the Latin order inverted the
meaning of the English. Thus *Dominum formidabunt adversarii
eius* becomes 'The Lord his adversaries shall dread.'[1]

The second version of Wycliffe's Bible, prepared after his
death by John Purvey, smoothes out these barbarisms and

---

[1] The passages are cited by Professor Deanesly in *The Significance of the
Lollard Bible* (University of London: The Athlone Press, 1951), p. 7.

contains many fine passages. It was completed some time between 1395 and 1397. The complete Bible did not appear *in print* until 1850. The New Testament, in the later edition, had, indeed, been issued once in the Eighteenth and twice in the Nineteenth Century. In 1850 the Oxford University Press brought out a complete edition of both versions in parallel columns, under the title *The Holy Bible, containing the Old and New Testaments with the Apocryphal Books in the earliest English versions made from the Latin Vulgate by John Wycliffe and his followers: Edited by the Rev. J. Forshall and Sir F. Madden.* The editors had taken twenty-two years over the work and examined a hundred and seventy different manuscripts. More have since come to light. This noble volume may be consulted in most larger reference libraries.

Why was not the Bible translated into English before? Few Englishmen are likely to be ignorant of the date 1066; but many ignore the consequences of the Conquest. The truth is that if a vernacular Bible had been prepared for the upper classes in England at any time within about two hundred years of 1066 it would have had to have been in French; and parts of the Scriptures in French were occasionally to be found in their houses. Almost the only versions which were available in Wycliffe's day were in Anglo-Saxon; and these were then about as incomprehensible as Latin. 'The only English Bibles which monastic libraries possessed, were, according to the catalogues, Anglo-Saxon gospel books or homilies on the gospels.'[1] Other versions, contemporary with Wycliffe, were in circulation; and there are gospels with interlinear paraphrases, and a North Midland edition of the Pauline epistles. Anglo-French and Middle English verse paraphrases of the Sunday Gospels had also been made at some time between 1250 and 1350.

We noticed, in the last chapter, that in the Middle Ages the book of the Bible which was best known was the Psalter.

[1] Deanesly, *The Lollard Bible*, p. 331.

If it was well known in Latin it came to be well known in English also. There were versions in verse and in prose—as, indeed, there are to this day. Of the prose versions the best known and the most influential was that written by Richard Rolle, who, like Wycliffe, was a native of North Yorkshire, but who lived for many years as a hermit at Hampole, near Doncaster, where he died, probably from the Black Death, in 1349. Copies were made in his life-time, and continued to be made, so that his book—with its lengthy commentary between the verses—became 'the standard English version of the Psalms.'[1]

Rolle was not, of course, of significance only or mainly as a translator. He was one of the earliest of English mystics, with an experience of unity with the living Christ expressed in language which may yet cause the spirit to kindle. He has been called the English Francis, with Margaret Kirkby, the recluse of Anderby—for whom he wrote his Psalter— playing the role of St. Clare.[2] The French historian Jusserand wrote of him, 'He is the first on the list of those lay preachers, of whom England has produced a number, whom an inward crisis brought back to God, and who roamed about the country as volunteer apostles, converting the simple, edifying the wise, and, alas! affording cause for laughter to the wicked. They are taken by good folk for saints, and for madmen by sceptics: such was the fate of Richard Rolle, of George Fox, of Bunyan and of Wesley; the same man lives on through the ages, and the same humanity heaps on him at once blessings and ridicule.'[3] Rolle might not have approved this succession; for he was not unorthodox; but it is significant that a prized possession of Sir John Oldcastle, who was put to death as a Lollard in 1417, was a copy of Rolle's Psalter. Oldcastle was also a

[1] *Ibid.*, p. 145.

[2] Evelyn Underhill, in the Introduction to *The Fire of Love and The Mending of Life or Rule of Living*, by Richard Rolle, edited by Frances M. M. Comper (2nd edition, London, 1920), pp. viii & ix.

[3] *A Literary History of the English People* from the Origins to the Renaissance (London, 1895), p. 216. Wesley would not have liked to have been called a lay preacher!

lay type which reappears in English history—caricatured
in an anti-Lollard poem of the period:

> Hit is unkyndly for a knight
>> That shuld a kinges castel kepe,
> To bable the Bible day and night
>> In restyng time when he shuld slepe.

When we press back in English history behind the Norman
Conquest it is to centuries of confusion and foreign invasion
lit up by a period of great missionary activity and of great
cultural eminence. If ever a country was transformed by the
coming of the Gospel it was England. Almost before the
conversion of its kingdoms was completed, the English were
taking the Christian message back to heathen parts of the
Continent, Willibrord (658–739) to the Low Countries and
Boniface (674–754) to Germany. Denmark, Norway and
Sweden, Iceland even, look back with gratitude to the
activities of English missionaries. Towards the end of the
Eighth Century, Charlemagne, who was later to restore the
Roman Empire, was looking around for the right man to
bring civilisation to his rude Frankish court and chose
Alcuin, the librarian of York. And already we have seen
that a copy of the Vulgate, which, despite its name, the
Codex Amiatinus, was written at Jarrow, is one of the greatest
and most richly adorned of all biblical manuscripts.

Sir F. M. Stenton has written of this remarkable cultural
efflorescence: 'At the middle of the seventh century there
was nothing to suggest the imminence of a great English
achievement in learning and literature. The strongest of
English kings was an obdurate heathen. The country was
distracted by wars which destroyed the peace of scholars,
and offered little but a succession of well-worn themes to
the makers of heroic verse. The Christian faith, which was to
carry imagination into new worlds, was only secure in the
extreme south-east of the island. Within a hundred years
England had become the home of a Christian culture which
influenced the whole development of letters and learning

in western Europe. The greatest historical work of the early middle ages had been written in a northern monastery, and the English poets had begun to give a permanent form to heroic traditions. There is nothing in European history closely parallel to this sudden development of a civilization by one of the most primitive peoples established within the ancient Roman empire.'[1]

At the heart of this achievement was the Bible. Even after the ferocious attacks of the Danes had brought a new darkness to the land, Alfred, the greatest of our early kings, knew that national life could not be re-fashioned by arms alone, but needed religion and learning. He represented all three in his own person. He translated *The Pastoral Care* of Gregory the Great, which was regarded for many centuries as a suitable manual of pastoral practice for a parish priest. He also translated the *Universal History* of Orosius and Bede's *Ecclesiastical History*. He wanted an educated clergy who would educate the young. When, at the end of his life, he promulgated his laws, he set them in a biblical frame by beginning with a translation of the account in chapters 20 to 23 of Exodus of how Moses gave the law, adding the 'Golden Rule' from Matthew and the passage in Acts 15 which describes the letter sent by the apostolic council at Jerusalem and links Christianity to the Mosaic law.

In the earlier period the shining light was Bede (673–735) a writer of European eminence. 'In an age when little was attempted beyond the registration of fact he had reached the conception of history.'[2] He lived his whole life around Jarrow. Here in the North was a scholar at home in Latin, Greek and Hebrew. One of his pupils, Cuthbert, later wrote in a letter to a friend a description of how Bede's last days were spent. On his bed he was busy with two English translations, of Excerpts from Isidore and of the Gospel of St. John. 'Ascension-day drew near. His illness increased,

---

[1] *Anglo-Saxon England* (2nd edition, Oxford, 1947), p. 177.
[2] Stenton, *op. cit.*, p. 187.

but he only laboured the more diligently. On the Wednesday, his scribe told him that one chapter alone remained, but feared that it might be painful for him to dictate. "It is easy", Bede replied, "take your pen and write quickly." The work was continued for some time. Then Bede directed Cuthbert to fetch his little treasures from his casket, pepper, scarves and incense, that he might distribute them among his friends. And so he passed the remainder of the day till evening in holy and cheerful conversation. His boy-scribe at last found an opportunity to remind him, with pious importunity, of his unfinished task: "One sentence, dear master, still remains unwritten." "Write quickly," he answered. The boy soon said, "It is completed now." "Well," Bede replied, "thou hast said the truth: all is ended. Take my head in thy hands, I would sit in the holy place in which I was wont to pray, that so sitting I may call upon my Father." Thereupon, resting on the floor of his cell, he chanted the *Gloria*, and his soul immediately passed away while the name of the Holy Spirit was on his lips.'[1]

It is a beautiful story: unfortunately no manuscript of Bede's translation has survived.

We think of Bede as a learned centre of a learned time: but he himself looked back to what he regarded as a time of greater learning. He recalled the days of Theodore of Tarsus, Archbishop of Canterbury from 669 to 690, 'the first archbishop,' wrote Bede, 'whom all the English church obeyed.' With the Greek Theodore came the North African, Hadrian, and together they set about the organization of the English Church. 'And forasmuch as both of them were well read both in sacred and in secular literature, they gathered a crowd of disciples, and there daily flowed from them rivers of knowledge to water the hearts of their hearers; and, together with the books of holy writ, they also taught them the arts of ecclesiastical poetry, astronomy and arithmetic. A testimony of which is, that there are still living at this day

[1] Abbreviated account in B. F. Westcott, *History of the English Bible* (2nd edition, London, 1872), p. 5.

some of their scholars, who are as well versed in the Greek
and Latin tongues as in their own, in which they were born.'[1]
In a sense Bede himself was one of these scholars, for the
Monastery at Jarrow had been founded by Benedict Biscop,
the Englishman who had first conducted Theodore from
Rome to Canterbury. He was later sent by Theodore
back to Rome and elsewhere, on more than one occasion, to
obtain supplies of books. It was to Jarrow that Biscop, or
the Abbot Ceolfrid, brought the Latin New Testament
manuscript which was later given to Boniface and is still
at his monastery of Fulda. It was from Jarrow that the
Codex Amiatinus was sent to the Pope.

Bede was a very erudite man: erudition is impossible
without access to libraries. It is clear that great numbers of
books were brought to England after its conversion: and in
the *scriptoria* of monasteries many were constantly being
copied for local use and for the missionaries who frequently
wrote from the Continent for fresh supplies. King Alfred
recalled, in about 890, how formerly 'foreigners came to
this land in search of wisdom and instruction, and we
should now have to get them from abroad if we wanted to
have them.' He did not believe that there existed south of
the Thames, at the time of his accession, a single Englishman 'able to translate a letter from Latin into English.
When I considered all this, I remembered also how I saw,
before it had all been ravaged and burnt, how the churches
throughout the whole of England stood filled with treasures
and books, and there was also a great multitude of God's
servants, but they had very little knowledge of the books,
for they could not understand anything of them, because
they were not written in their own language.'[2] Alcuin's
library at York was probably the finest in Western Europe.
But this also perished by fire in 1069, a part of the 'harrying'
of the rebellious North by William the Conqueror.

It was the policy—perhaps as much unconscious as

---

[1] *Ecclesiastical History*, Bk. IV, Ch. 2, Everyman edition, p. 164.
[2] Jusserand, *op. cit.*, p. 81.

5

conscious—of the Norman ruling classes to minimize the intellectual and cultural achievements of pre-Conquest days. For them the earlier English were illiterate and boorish. Yet on the Continent the works of Bede were being assiduously transcribed and he was being regarded as one of the Fathers of the Church. Anglo-Saxon manuscripts also continued to be read and copied throughout the earlier medieval period: in the later they remained in monastery libraries, unread because hardly understood. It is thought that the oldest of these now in existence is one in the Library of Corpus Christi College, Cambridge, written by an unknown Aelfric, a monk of Bath early in the Tenth Century. It was in the Tenth Century that Aldred added to the Lindisfarne Gospels his gloss, or interlinear translation. This version was in Northumbrian, or Northern English: a similar gloss into Mercian, or Midlands English, was made a little later in what are known as the Rushworth Gospels, which are now in the Bodleian Library. A better-known Aelfric (*c.* 950–*c.* 1020), Abbot of Eynsham, in Oxfordshire, the most important scholar of his time, who wrote considerably in Latin and English, made a translation of selections from the Old Testament. A copy of this exists at Oxford and another in the British Museum.[1]

Christianity was brought to England by missionaries, both from the South and the North. We have seen that they brought learning with them, and books, its indispensable basis; and that before very long there were some English clergy who were not only competent in Latin but had some knowledge of Greek and even Hebrew. Did they immediately render the Scriptures into Anglo-Saxon? The answer, in Professor Deanesly's words is that there is 'no evidence that a complete translation, even of the four gospels, was made till the time of Aelfric, in the eleventh century, or that biblical translations were used at all in the Anglo-Saxon period for the regular instruction

---

[1] There was a third Aelfric, Archbishop of Canterbury from 995 to 1005, to whom Sir Frederic Kenyon appears to have attributed this translation. See *Our Bible and the Ancient Manuscripts* (4th edition, 1939), p. 199.

of monks, priests or laity. Generally speaking, the text of
the Bible was studied only by the monks, and it was studied
in Latin.'[1] It is to be noticed that the reference here is to
the text of the Bible, not to its content as it might be expounded by priests and teachers. Likely lads, who might
become candidates for ordination, were taught Latin:
the unlearned were told the Bible stories and given moral
instruction, which came in time to be supported by pictures
and plays, to say nothing of the drama of the Mass itself.

They also used poetry. It is sometimes difficult for us to
realize the capacity for learning by heart possessed by many
people in an age less verbally oppressed than our own. As
late as 1542 Bishop Bonner ordered all the priests of the
Diocese of London to learn the whole New Testament by
heart. Ten years later Archbishop Holgate enjoined that
all the vicars choral of York, who were under forty years of
age, should commit to memory every week, 'One chapter
of Sancte Poule's Epistles in Latyne, after the translation of
Erasmus, begynnynge at the first chapiter of the Epistle
to the Romanes; and that the queresters do learn withoute
booke every weke, or at leaste every fourtenighte, one
chapiter of the Gospells, and th'Acctes of the Apostles to
th'ende, in th'Enlishe tonge, begynnynge at the firste
chapitour of Sancte Matheue.'[2] For simple folk, in earlier
days, the Gospel story was turned into rhyme. Aldhelm,
Abbot of Malmesbury and later the first Bishop of Sher-
borne, a man learned in Latin, with some knowledge also
of Greek and Hebrew, 'beyond comparison the most learned

---

[1] *The Lollard Bible*, p. 132. This has remained the missionary policy of the
Roman Church. 'It is well known that the number of languages in which some
portion of the Scriptures exists now considerably exceeds one thousand. The
vast majority of these translations has been made in connection with the
missionary work of the non-Roman Churches of the west. There is agreement
among all the missionary agencies of the various confessions that the production of the Scriptures in the language of the people at the earliest possible date
is one of the indispensable foundations of the Christian society. This is one of
the clearest differences between Roman and non-Roman missionary work.
Very early examples of Roman versions of the Scriptures in Chinese exist;
but these are exceptions to an otherwise almost unvarying practice, that the
Scriptures are not put into the hands of the ordinary members of that Church.'
Stephen Neill, *The Christian Society* (London, 1952), p. 197.
[2] Quoted, Frederick Harrison, *Life in a Medieval College* (London, 1952), p. 207.

and ingenious western scholar of the late seventh century', was also a poet in his own language. William of Malmesbury records how he composed a trivial song in English, interlarded with passages from Scripture, and that, disguised as a wandering minstrel, he sang it upon a bridge leading from the town as truants from Mass made their way into the country.

Bede also wrote to Egbert, Archbishop of York, in 734, to impress the importance of everyone, lay and clerical alike, having the Apostles' Creed and the Lord's Prayer firmly in their memories, saying that he had often presented to uneducated priests the Creed and the Paternoster translated into English.[1] Bede himself also tells the story of the herdsman Caedmon, who rendered the Bible story in rhymes which his fellows could remember and understand; and who won for himself in later centuries the title of the father of English poetry.

Caedmon worked at the great monastery at Whitby, where St. Hilda presided over a double community of men and women. Bede tells us that until an advanced age 'he had never learned anything of versifying; for which reason being sometimes at entertainment, when it was agreed for the sake of mirth that all present should sing in their turns, when he saw the instrument come towards him, he rose up from table and returned home.' But once, when this had happened, he had a vision in the stable where he was sleeping. 'A person appeared to him in his sleep, and saluting him by his name, said, "Caedmon, sing some song to me".' He found he was able to do it, indeed 'to praise the Maker of the heavenly kingdom, the power of the Creator and his counsel, the deeds of the Father of glory.' The next day the Abbess and her counsellors were persuaded that he had indeed received a grace from God; and he was taken into the monastery as a brother.

An interesting process now began. The learned men of the monastery taught Caedmon passages from Scripture:

[1] J. W. Adamson, *The Illiterate Anglo-Saxon*, p. 6.

he turned them into verse. 'Thus Caedmon, keeping in mind all he heard, and as it were chewing the cud, converted the same into the most harmonious verse; and sweetly repeating the same, made his masters in their turn his hearers. He sang the creation of the world, the origin of man, and all the history of Genesis: and made many verses on the departure of the children of Israel out of Egypt, and their entering into the land of promise, with many histories from holy writ; the incarnation, passion, resurrection of our Lord, and his ascension into heaven; the coming of the Holy Ghost, and the preaching of the apostles; also the terror of future judgment, the horror of the pains of hell, and the delights of heaven; besides many more about the Divine benefits and judgments, by which he endeavoured to turn away all men from the love of vice, and to excite in them the love of, and application to, good actions.'[1]

This is indeed a synopsis of early preaching at its best. Through the genius of Caedmon, there were valleys in England, as round Jerome's Bethlehem, where as the ploughman drove his share, he sang his alleluia, where the sweating reaper diverted himself with psalms and the shepherds sang them also as they came in from the hills.

[1] Bede, *op. cit.*, Bk. IV, ch. XXIV; pp. 206, 207.

Chapter Six

BACK TO THE MISSIONARIES – II

A WITTY and distinguished Welshman represented Henry II at the third Lateran Council, called by Pope Alexander III in 1179. This was Walter Map, who is of interest to historians of literature because of the part he is believed to have played in the composition of some portions of the cycle of Arthurian romances. In his reminiscences he described how a deputation of Waldensians came to the Council. 'They were simple and illiterate men,' he wrote, 'named after their leader Waldo, who was a citizen of Lyons on the Rhone; and they presented to the Lord pope a book written in the French tongue, in which were contained a text and gloss on the psalter and on very many other books of both testaments. These besought with great urgency that authority to preach should be confirmed to them, for they thought themselves expert, when they were scarcely learned at all. Shall not therefore the Word given to the unlearned be as *pearls before swine*?'

The Welshman's reaction to this novelty followed traditional lines. So did Papal policy. Waldo's followers were excommunicated in 1185, and condemned once again by the fourth Lateran Council in 1215. This was not, of course, only because of their Bible reading; but it will be remembered that Jean Gerson later found the source of their errors in 'this pestiferous root'. In many ways the Waldensians foreshadowed later Protestants and Puritans and the smaller sects of to-day. Despite much oppression, a small Waldensian Church has maintained a vigorous life in the Alpine valleys of Italy down to the present day. But Waldensian influence was much more widespread. They inspired similar movements in medieval Germany: and when the German Bible was first printed the text was almost

certainly of Waldensian origin. Even translations of the
Bible used in Italian nunneries at the time of the Reformation have been traced back to Waldensian texts.[1]

The Waldensians spread among the illiterate classes.
Their people could not read. This was not to say that they
could not learn. An inquisitor giving evidence at Béziers in
1246 declared: 'I myself have seen a young cowherd, who
for the space of only a year stayed in the house of a certain
Waldensian heretic, who learned by heart and retained
with such diligent attention and careful repetition in his
mind what he had heard that within that year he had
learnt and remembered forty of the Sunday gospels (without
counting the feast days), and he had learnt all these in his
own tongue word for word, apart from other words of
sermons and prayers.'[2] In about 1260 an inquisitor of Passau
wrote a tract on heresy, attacking the Waldensians in
particular under six heads. The third was 'that they have
translated the New and Old Testament into the vulgar
tongue and this they teach and learn. For I have heard and
seen a certain unlettered countryman who used to recite
Job word for word, and many others who knew the whole
New Testament perfectly.'[3]

It is no wonder that the men of the Reformation felt
kinship with these pioneers, nor that John Milton should be
stung to fierce verse at the news of yet another attempt to
stamp out this pristine Protestantism:

> Avenge, O Lord! Thy slaughter'd Saints, whose bones
> Lie scatter'd on the Alpine mountains cold;
> Even them who kept Thy truth so pure of old,
> Even when our fathers worshipt stocks and stones.

The fourth line expresses a condemnation of the whole
medieval past as idolatrous which few would endorse
to-day. The men of the Seventeenth Century saw most
things in black and white: the first translations of the Bible

[1] Deanesly, *The Lollard Bible*, pp. 64, 15.
[2] *Ibid.*, p. 38.
[3] *Ibid.*, p. 64.

into the language of the people represented for them the first bright rays of light piercing a black night. But we may recall that the Church authorities regarded this obscurity as good and not evil. Pope Gregory VII had written to Vratislaus, King of Bohemia, in 1079 to restrain the circulation of the Scriptures in Slavonic. 'For it is clear to those who reflect often upon it, that not without reason has it pleased Almighty God that holy scripture should be a secret in certain places lest, if it were plainly apparent to all men, perchance it would be little esteemed and be subject to disrespect; or it might be falsely understood by those of mediocre learning, and lead to error.'[1]

At an earlier time this translation had won papal approval. It was the result of the great missionary work in the Ninth Century of two Greek brothers from Salonika, Constantine —who took the name of Cyril shortly before his death at Rome in 869—and Methodius. Their work was mainly in Moravia, where they established a seminary for priests whom they instructed in a Slavonic version of the liturgy, which won the approval of Popes Adrian II and John VIII. For this—and for their scriptural translations—they chose the Macedo-Bulgarian dialect. Constantine created a new form of alphabet, based largely on Greek characters, though probably influenced by Latin and Hebrew forms. This is often called Cyrillic, from the name he adopted. Thus he gave to the Slav Church both a ritual language and an alphabet: and this has contributed in no small measure to the separation of Eastern Europe from the civilisation of the West. The Cyrillic characters are still used in Russia and Bulgaria and parts of Yugoslavia.

The Slavonic version has only been partially preserved. Its Old Testament is mainly based on the Greek; but in parts there are indications that Hebrew has been used, and in parts Latin.

Much earlier than this Bishop Ulfilas (312–380) had carried through an even more exacting task by translating

---

[1] *Ibid.*, p. 24.

the Bible into Gothic for the benefit of the Gothic tribes
then moving through Bulgaria and Serbia. The remains
of his version are the only remains of the Gothic language
which have come down to us. They are of interest to
Englishmen, for when transcribed into modern characters
a similarity may be discerned with the English language.
Thus the Lord's Prayer begins:

> Atta unsar thu in himinam, weihnai namo thein
> Father *our thou in heaven,* be hallowed *name thine*

The English words in italics are of the same origin as the
Gothic ones which they translate.[1] Dr. Latourette has
written of Ulfilas that 'what may have been his most note-
worthy achievement was his translation of a large part of
the Bible into the Gothic tongue. For this purpose he is
said to have devised an alphabet. If that be true, we have
here what is probably the first or the second instance of
what has since happened to hundreds of tongues—their
reduction to writing by Christian missionaries and the
translation into them by that medium of a part or all of
the Scriptures.'[2] The same writer has told us that this has
been the reason for the reduction to writing of the majority
of the languages of the world—many of them unknown by
name to ordinary educated people, because the people or
tribe they serve is small and obscure. The work is still
going on. The basis of the missionary task remains
the same.

The Gothic Version, like the Slavonic, was based upon
the Greek. But as the Goths moved into Italy they took their
Bible with them. Bilingual codices began to appear—of
which some traces remain—with Gothic in one column and
Latin in the other. Souter believes that an Old Latin manuscript was taken and partly corrected to the Vulgate; and
that it was then altered to fit the renderings and readings
of the Gothic (and through the Gothic, of course, to the

---

[1] The Lord's Prayer is set out in this way in full by Henry Bradley, in *The
Goths* (The Story of the Nations series), London 1888, p. 62.

[2] *A History of the Expansion of Christianity,* vol. i, p. 214.

Greek).[1] One magnificent manuscript of part of the Bible of Ulfilas is in the Library of the University of Upsala. It was found in the library of the monastery at Werden in Germany but was taken to Sweden as part of the booty from the Thirty Years' War. In 1662 it was bought by the Swedish Count de la Gardie, who had it bound in silver. The book is itself written in silver letters on purple stained vellum; and is appropriately known as the *Codex Argenteus*. It was probably written in North Italy in the sixth century.

Christian missionaries did not, of course, go to Europe only, as anyone brought up on the missionary journeys of Saint Paul knows very well. Throughout his work, however, there were few occasions when a knowledge of Greek was not sufficient.[2] Since the conquests of Alexander the Great —between 336 and 323 B.C.—Greek had become a second language for all people in the Near East who had any pretensions to education. In Egypt Alexandria was a Greek-speaking city—with a large population of Jews for whom the Old Testament had to be translated into Greek. The native Egyptians seemed unimportant and their needs were little considered. That they chattered away in some tongue of their own did not matter to their European overlords so long as they knew enough of Greek or Latin to obey orders and ship the necessary grain for the hungry mouths of Italy.

In time, however, Christianity made its way among these people too, and the lists of those who were martyred in Egypt in the great persecution of Diocletian in A.D. 303 contain numerous Egyptian names. Versions of Scripture began to appear in various dialects of Coptic, the ancient language of Egypt, which, from the second century began to be written in Greek characters, with the addition of six letters to represent sounds not found in Greek. There was the Bohairic dialect, spoken in the Nile Delta, the Sahidic dialect spoken in Upper Egypt, and various dialects spoken

[1] *The Text and Canon of the New Testament*, p. 44.
[2] That it was awkward occasionally not to know the local language is indicated by Acts 14.8–18.

in the district known as the Fayyum. In the Nile Delta
Greek was so long dominant that it is probable that there
was no translation into Bohairic until the Fourth Century.
This is still the official Bible of the Coptic Church: it is the
only complete version, and has many manuscripts, though
many of them are late. G. W. Horner produced a version
of the Bohairic New Testament for the Clarendon Press
between 1898 and 1905 which used forty-six manuscripts
for the Gospels and thirty-four for the other books. Some of
the best manuscripts of the Bohairic are in the Bodleian
Library and in the British Museum.

The Sahidic version is earlier. Its early existence is indicated
by the fact that Pachomius, the great organiser of monas-
ticism in Egypt at the beginning of the Fourth Century,
required his monks—who were ordinary Egyptians—to be
diligent in the study of the Scriptures; and there is no
indication that they had to learn Greek first. Earlier than
this, St. Anthony, who was born about 250, is recorded to
have been greatly impressed by hearing the Scriptures
read in church at the age of twenty. He did not know
Greek: what he heard may have been from a Sahidic version
or may have been a verbal translation given by the reader.
The Sahidic comes from an area where Greek was never
so dominant as it was in the Nile Delta. It has been pieced
together from many fragments. The Clarendon Press
issued a critical version of the Sahidic Gospels, in three
volumes, edited by G. W. Horner, in 1911. He was able
to give a complete text of the Gospels, except thirteen
verses in Matthew, thirty-five in Mark, and three in Luke;
but of these fifty-one missing verses small parts were available
of all but fourteen. The fact that the district in which Sahidic
was spoken is fairly isolated has meant that the manuscripts
have been little adulterated by outside influences. 'A
papyrus containing portions of Deuteronomy, Jonah, and
Acts, and forming part of a codex from a date not later
than the middle of the fourth century A.D. has a text which
is in precise agreement with Coptic manuscripts of the

twelfth and thirteenth centuries.'[1] Behind the Coptic versions there lies the Greek.

The penetration of Christianity further South into Ethiopia resulted in the production of an Ethiopic version of the Scriptures. The Old Testament version was probably made in the Fourth Century A.D. and the New Testament about 600 A.D. That the Old Testament translation is the earlier is a reminder that it is the Bible of the Falashas also, the remarkable community of African Jews whose members claim to be descended from immigrants into the country in the times of Solomon and the Queen of Sheba. Complete versions of both Testaments exist in manuscript; but no manuscript is early and they have been little studied. The Greek version appears to lie behind them; but some scholars think that although the original translation was made from the Greek the present manuscripts go back to translations from Coptic and Arabic in the Fourteenth Century. The Ethiopic Old Testament contains a number of books which are neither in the Hebrew Old Testament nor in the Apocrypha. One of these—the Book of Enoch—has great interest for scholars. It is quoted in the fourteenth verse of Jude, and echoed elsewhere in that short Epistle. The late R. H. Charles once wrote that 'the influence of Enoch on the New Testament has been greater than that of all the other apocryphal and pseudepigraphical books taken together.' The book was quite lost until James Bruce brought back some manuscripts from Abyssinia in 1773: it was first edited in 1821 by Archbishop Laurence. Portions of the book in Greek were discovered in 1886 and 1931. But there is yet no complete Greek version: for the middle chapters scholars are dependent on the Ethiopic.

In the time of Jesus Hebrew was, except for Church purposes, a dead language. In Palestine, of course, Church purposes were largely dominant throughout the country. The Jews were a literate people and the basis of learning to

[1] Bleddyn J. Roberts, *The Old Testament Text and Versions* (Cardiff, 1951), p. 230.

read was the Hebrew Bible. Nevertheless Hebrew was not
a language spoken in the streets. There men spoke Aramaic:
that Jesus spoke it is evidenced by His own reported words,
Talitha Cumi and *Eli, Eli, lama sabachthani.* It would be
expected that the Gospels would circulate in the language
He spoke. That they were written in this language is the
conclusion of some scholars. Irenaeus, indeed, in the
Second Century, wrote that the First Gospel was written
by Matthew 'among the Hebrews in their own language,
while Peter and Paul were preaching and founding the
Church at Rome.' This tradition probably goes back to an
enigmatic statement by Papias—one who lived early enough
to have known those who had themselves heard and known
the Apostles—that 'Matthew composed the oracles in the
Hebrew language, and each one interpreted them as he
could.' What were 'the oracles'? Some think a collection of
proof-texts from the Old Testament; others the sayings of
Jesus. But few scholars outside the Roman Church now
believe that St. Matthew was the first Gospel: most are
convinced that—as it exists to-day—it is essentially a
Greek book, partly dependent upon two Greek sources,
one of which has been lost, but the other of which is St.
Mark; and that these two sources were also used by St. Luke.

It should, however, be remembered that the late Professor Burney of Oxford believed that the Fourth Gospel
was a translation from the Aramaic. Professor Torrey, of
Yale, goes further and is convinced that 'there is clear and
complete evidence that the Gospels of Matthew, Mark,
and John were composed in Aramaic on the basis of diverse
written material widespread in Palestine, and that our
Greek is the result of literal translation.' These supposed
Aramaic Gospels have however entirely perished. 'The
Greek of our Gospels,' he adds, 'with its thoroughly Semitic
idiom, is the result not only of literal translation, but often
of mistranslation, never extensive, but sometimes very disturbing. Thanks to the ancient word-for-word method of
rendering, the cause of the trouble is almost always evident

when an exact Semitic metaphrase of the Greek is made.'[1]
The case is persuasively argued; but few scholars are convinced. Some illumination can, indeed, be gained by this
method of translating the sayings of Jesus back into Aramaic
to discover whether His original words have been mis-
translated by the Evangelists or those who lay behind them.
But that the Gospels as we have them are Greek books,
the first three of which are closely interrelated even in tiny
Greek particles—few now doubt.[2]

The dominance of Palestine by Aramaic is very remarkable; for it was originally the language of those who
took the Hebrews captive to Babylon in the Sixth Century
B.C. Yet the Palestine Jews ultimately spoke the language
of their overlords with a difference; and the term Aramaic
is usually confined to the Western version of the language,
while the form still spoken in the Euphrates valley—it is
still a living language in the neighbourhood of Mosul—is
called Syriac. There are hardly any Palestinian manuscripts of the Scriptures existing—only various parts of a
lectionary containing biblical extracts. The Syriac versions
are however most important.

What became 'the Vulgate of the Syriac-speaking Church'
is the version known as the *Peshitta*. The word means 'simple'
or 'plain'. The origins of this version are unfortunately not
very simple. Its Old Testament shows the influence both of
Hebrew and Greek. Some believe that it should be dated
within the Christian era; others that it is earlier. The
British Museum possesses a manuscript of the Pentateuch
in this version which is the oldest copy of the Bible in any
language of which the exact date is known. It is dated
'in the year of the Greeks, 775', which is equivalent to
A.D. 442.[3]

---

[1] *The Four Gospels: A New Translation.* Preface ix, x.

[2] Learned men who translate the Gospels back into Aramaic are beset by
many pitfalls. Streeter noted that when Torrey reviewed Burney's book 'he
assents to the general proposition that the Gospel is a translation from the
Aramaic, but rejects practically all the alleged mistranslations on which
Dr. Burney's argument largely rests. He then proceeds to offer another set of
"mistranslations" of his own discovering.' *The Four Gospels*, p. 400, n.2.

[3] Roberts, *op. cit.*, p. 223.

The New Testament version was made at the instigation of Rabbula, who was Bishop of Edessa from 401 to 435. Earlier Syriac versions were compared with Greek manuscripts in use in Constantinople and the Syriac smoothed out to approximate to the Greek. This process has removed much of the value of the *Peshitta* as an independent witness: it contains little which is not to be found in Greek manuscripts. The *Peshitta* Bible, which is the authorised version of the still existing Assyrian Church, does not contain 2 and 3 John, 2 Peter, Jude or Revelation.

There were later revisions of the Syriac New Testament to make it a more exact rendering of the Greek. What is more important is that manuscripts of the Old Syriac Gospels— the text which lies behind the Peshitta and has not been smoothed out to suit the Greek—have been discovered. The Curetonian MSS. are eighty leaves of the Gospels, called after Dr. Cureton of the British Museum who published them in 1858. This caused a great stir, as he claimed that the version contained the actual words of Jesus in the very language which He spoke. This has not been accepted; but the Curetonian MSS. are regarded as representing a most important text of great antiquity. In 1892 two ladies from Cambridge, Mrs. Lewis and her sister Mrs. Gibson, visited the Monastery on Mount Sinai where Tischendorf had discovered the *Codex Sinaiticus* and Professor Rendel Harris the lost *Apology of Aristides*. These ladies—the date was 1892 and the place Mount Sinai—photographed a number of manuscripts. One was a 'palimpsest' in which, below Greek writing, were earlier Syriac characters. Professor Burkitt and others in Cambridge recognised that here was another Old Syriac find. The date they suggested was A.D. 200.

The version of the Gospels represented, in different ways, by these finds, is entitled *The Gospel of the Separated Ones*. This does not mean that they contain the Gospel of a separated people; but that the Gospel story is separated into Matthew, Mark, Luke and John. This distinguishes it from the form in which it was ordinarily known by Syriac-speaking Christians. This was in a kind of harmony of the Gospels—prepared on the basis of St. John by a scissors and paste method—which was known as the *Diatessaron*. (The Greek name means 'By Four'.) This was made around A.D. 170 by a much travelled native of Mesopotamia called Tatian. He almost certainly made his harmony in Greek and then translated it into Syriac. This quickly became, and long remained, the form in which the Gospels were read in Syriac-speaking churches and commented upon by Syriac-speaking theologians. Yet it has been lost. 'It may safely be said', wrote Alexander Souter, 'that the original Greek of Tatian's book is a more desirable possession for the textual critic of the Gospels than almost anything else yet undiscovered: the Syriac in its original form would be only less valuable.'[1]

When a book cannot be found people are likely to say that it does not exist. In 1876 the author of *Supernatural Religion* boldly denied the existence of the *Diatessaron*. The Armenian community in Venice had however, as early as 1836, published an Armenian version of the works of the Fourth-Century St. Ephraem of Syria, including a commentary upon the *Diatessaron*, from which many quotations were made. Few people read Armenian; and the publication passed unnoticed by Western scholars. In 1876 a Latin version was issued; but even this was not noticed immediately: not so very many people read Latin. In 1880, however, attention was drawn to it by the American scholar, Dr. Ezra Abbott, and the existence of the *Diatessaron* decisively proved. Later there were discovered—and published in 1888—two manuscripts of a translation of the *Diatessaron* into Arabic which had been made by a monk in the Eleventh Century.

A still later discovery must be recounted in the words of the late Sir Frederic Kenyon, to whom this account owes so much:

[1] *Op. cit.*, p. 56.

In 1920 British troops were in occupation at a place called Salihiyah on the western bank of the upper Euphrates, and there some English officers discovered the remains of a Roman fortress, on the walls of which were remains of ancient paintings. They reported their find to head-quarters, and Miss Gertrude Bell, realising their importance, urged the American archæologist Professor J. H. Breasted to visit the site. The troops were, however, on the eve of being withdrawn, and Professor Breasted was only able to have a single day there. Without that one day, all interest in the site might have been lost; but Professor Breasted and his colleagues were able to realise the value of the paintings and to take notes and photographs, and subsequently, when Salihiyah had come within the area of the French mandate, detailed excavations were undertaken by Professor Franz Cumont and Professor Breasted, subsequently continued by Yale University, under the direction of Professor M. Rostovzeff. These excavations revealed that the site was that of Dura-Europos, a Roman fortified frontier city, which after various vicissitudes had been captured by the Persians in A.D. 256. Just before the final siege, the walls had been strengthened by a huge ramp on the inside, which sealed up the ruins of a quantity of buildings, including a Christian Church and a Jewish synagogue; and among them was a room with a number of papyrus and vellum fragments. One of these vellum fragments, when examined at Yale in 1933, proved to contain fourteen imperfect lines of the Diatessaron in Greek. The document is necessarily earlier than A.D. 256, and may be assigned with certainty to the first half of the third century.[1]

Fourteen lines are hardly Souter's desideratum. But their importance is very great.

These chapters have been headed 'Back to the Missionaries' and mention has been made of Edessa. This town on

---

[1] *Our Bible and the Ancient Manuscripts* (fourth edition, 1939), p. 159.

6

the Euphrates was an early oasis of Christianity among heathens. Indeed there is an apocryphal correspondence between Jesus and its king. Eusebius wrote that the entire city had been Christian from the apostolic age to his own time (264–340). That is an obvious exaggeration. But, as Harnack points out, it must be true of the age of which he wrote; and 'The Christian city of Edessa probably had a larger percentage of Christians among its population than any of the larger towns during the period previous to Constantine.' Missionary work and literary labours have a way of going together.

Chapter Seven

THE GREAT CODICES

THERE have been many crises in the history of Christianity. Few have been greater than that initiated at Nicomedia, the new city built by the Emperor Diocletian as his headquarters, on the eastern coast of the Sea of Marmora, on February 23rd, 303. By the Emperor's orders a church was first destroyed; and soon edicts against the profession of Christianity were being posted upon the hoardings—and as quickly pulled down. The 'persecution of Diocletian' which began in this way was startling and unexpected. For a long time the Church had been undisturbed: a measure of toleration had encouraged its growth. The Roman Empire was now 'overspread by a vast confederation of strongly organised churches assembling for elaborate services, often in splendid buildings with overflowing congregations.'[1] To an Emperor whose domains were only held together by desperate military contrivance this came to look very like a fifth column everywhere actively at work.[2] It must be suppressed.

This last great persecution by the Roman Empire was slow in coming and it was some time before its full seriousness was felt. Then it had become violent. Yet throughout its course there appears to have been a realisation that the main enemy which the state had to face was neither the Christian buildings nor even the Christians themselves but the books which they possessed. If these were not destroyed they might be like buried seeds and put forth new life later on. That indeed happened. Many copies of the Scriptures were destroyed. When the persecution died down and discipline was restored to the Church the most important

[1] H. M. Gwatkin, *Early Church History* (London, 1909), vol. i, p. 170.
[2] See R. H. Barrow, *The Romans* (London, Penguin Books, 1949), p. 186.

moral problem was what should be done about the *tradi-tores*, who had 'handed over' sacred books for destruction. Biblical studies are poorer in the material at their disposal because of the persecution of Diocletian. But not all were *traditores*. Copies of the Scriptures were buried and hidden and then brought out again. This was the last great persecution. Its failure led to the victory of the Church. In 306 Constantine—later known to history as the first Christian Emperor—was hailed as Augustus by his troops at York. In 312 he was greeted with the same title by the Senate in Rome. In 313 there was issued the Edict of Milan proclaiming freedom of worship. In 324 Constantine became sole Emperor.

The victory of the Church was complete. Christianity now was not merely a tolerated religion but one which had special official approval. It became fashionable to join the Church. There was, naturally, need for many more Church buildings. There was also need for many more Bibles.

The centre of gravity in the Empire was no longer at Rome but much further East. Diocletian had made Nicomedia his virtual capital. Constantine now looked across the waters to the ancient city of Byzantium. This was rebuilt as a new Rome. For the churches in this new city of Constantinople the Emperor himself, in A.D. 332, ordered fifty vellum Bibles from Eusebius of Caesarea: and in the writings of Eusebius a copy of the letter has been preserved. It reads as follows:

I have thought it expedient to instruct your Intelligence that you should command to be written fifty volumes on prepared vellum, easy to read and conveniently portable, by professional scribes with an exact understanding of their craft—volumes, that is to say, of the Holy Scriptures, the provision and use of which is, as you are aware, most necessary for the instruction of the Church. Letters have been dispatched from our Clemency to the accountant of the province, advising him to supply everything requisite for the production of the books, and it will be your care to ensure that they are prepared as quickly as possible. Using the authority of this letter you should commandeer two public carriages for their transport, for by such means will these fine volumes be most readily brought before our eyes, this duty being performed by one of the deacons of your church, who on reaching our presence will experience our liberality.[1]

It would be exciting if we could claim that in some museum there was to be found one of the actual Bibles ordered by Constantine for the churches in his new capital. No such claim can be made. What we can say, however, is that books of this character and date do exist. They are our primary authority for the text of the Greek Bible.

A large volume of the kind ordered by Constantine is called a *codex*. The word is used to describe a manuscript which in shape and appearance is like a modern book—though very much larger than most. (A leaf of the *Codex Sinaiticus* measures fifteen inches in height by thirteen and a half in breadth; one from the *Codex Alexandrinus* is rather smaller.) It is in the period of which we are now thinking that the codex form finally won the victory over the earlier roll; and vellum its victory over the earlier papyrus. It was long thought that there were no papyrus codices; but the comparatively recent discovery of the Chester Beatty Papyri has revealed that this far less durable material, made from the pith of a Nile valley reed, much more like modern paper, was also sometimes made up in the codex form.

Vellum—or parchment—is made from the skin of sheep or of goats. (Both animals sometimes make their contribution to one volume.) Though both sides of a sheet of vellum are written upon, the outer 'hair side', by reason of its roughness, presents greater difficulty to the scribe than the smoother 'flesh side'. A method of book construction

[1] Quoted in *The Codex Sinaiticus and the Codex Alexandrinus* (British Museum, 1951), p. 21.

was evolved so that pages opened flesh-side to flesh-side and hair-side to hair-side throughout. Very careful measurements were made to ensure a neat appearance of the page and an economical use of the costly materials employed. Lines were ruled and pricks made through the folded sheets of vellum (on the parts where writing would later make these marks almost invisible) to guide the scribe. This accounts for the attractive regularity of the writing in the great codices which have survived. In *Codex Sinaiticus*, for example, each page was ruled with four narrow columns usually containing forty-eight lines apiece. In the poetical books of the Old Testament, however, the arrangement was different. The writing was in two columns and the use of indented lines emphasised the verse structure. The use of a rather similar scheme in the printing of the Revised Version, whereby verse is easily distinguishable from prose, was thus a return to an early practice.

The widespread adoption of Christianity throughout the Roman Empire in the Fourth Century led, as we have seen, to a great demand for the materials of Christian instruction. Other cities emulated Constantinople in endeavouring to secure the best copies which money could buy. In earlier days a Church which possessed the Scriptures would own them in parts. The New Testament would be in one section for the Gospels, a second section for the Epistles of St. Paul. A third section headed Acts would also contain, very likely, the other New Testament Epistles, or some of them: and there might be a fourth section containing the Revelation. But now whole Bibles were made, to become, not only a means of instruction but a source of ecclesiastical and civic pride.

Three imposing volumes have survived—none of them complete—from this period, the *Codex Vaticanus*, the *Codex Sinaiticus* and the *Codex Alexandrinus*. The first, as its name implies, is in the Library of the Vatican, where it has been at least since 1481, the date of a catalogue in which it is listed. *Codex Sinaiticus* is in the British Museum. It was bought in 1933 from the Soviet Government for £100,000. The British Government agreed to pay £1 for every £1 raised by the Museum; but so successful was the appeal that the Museum was able to pay more than its agreed quota. (This is one happy memory of the year in which Hitler came to power!) The *Codex Alexandrinus* is also in the British Museum. It reached England in 1627. Sir Thomas Roe, English Ambassador to Turkey, came into close contact with the Greek Patriarch, Cyril Lucar, whom he was able to help, more particularly in his struggles against the pretensions of the Roman Church, which had the support of the French Ambassador. In return Lucar promised to help the Ambassador in his search for manuscripts which scholars in England were anxious to obtain. In 1625 Roe wrote to the Earl of Arundel describing how there had been handed over to him for the King of England 'an autographall bible intire, written by the hand of Tecla the protomartyr of the Greekes, that liued in the tyme of St. Paul; and he doth auerr yt to be true and authenticall, of his owne writing, and the greatest antiquitye of the Greeke church.' Meanwhile James I, for whom the present was intended, died: but Lucar gave it again on January 1st, 1627, as a New Year's present for the new King, Charles I.[1]

There is also in England the famous *Codex Bezae*, which may date from the Sixth or the Fifth Century. It is called after the scholar Theodore Beza, by whom it was owned and used, and who presented it to the University of Cambridge in 1581. It is now in the University Library. Beza obtained it in Lyons in 1562, but no one knows where it originally came from. It is the first example of a Bible in two languages, with the Greek and Latin side by side. This indicates that it originated in the West, where Latin was the dominant language: the actual style of writing indicates that it did not come from one of the great centres of scribal industry, such as Alexandria or Rome. It is smaller than the other codices described, each page measuring ten by eight

---

[1] *Ibid.*, p. 28.

inches. The writing is in a single column, the Greek on the left-hand page and the Latin on the right. It contains the Gospels and Acts only. What makes it of particular interest is the considerable number of variations it contains from other texts. In some places the Latin version has been accommodated to the Greek: in others the reverse process has taken place. There are, as might be expected, many minor variations. But there are also additions and omissions of a kind which is unique. Thus in Luke 6, in place of verse 5, it records this incident, which is found nowhere else: 'On the same day, seeing one working on the sabbath day, he said unto him, Man, if thou knowest what thou doest, blessed art thou: but if thou knowest not, thou art accursed and a transgressor of the law.' Was this an invention, or a genuine saying of Jesus, independently preserved? Some would like to think that it was the latter.

These great manuscripts are called uncials, because they were written in capital letters throughout. When a running hand was later adopted the resulting manuscripts are called cursives or minuscules. The uncials are similarly referred to by capital letters—whether Roman letters or Hebrew or Greek. *Codex Vaticanus* is known as B, *Codex Sinaiticus* is known by the Hebrew letter א (*aleph*), *Codex Alexandrinus* is A, *Codex Bezae* is D, and the manuscript discovered in 1913 at Koridethi beyond the Black Sea is known by the Greek capital letter *theta* Θ. In uncial writing no break was made between the words and there were a number of contractions. It is as if the opening verse of St. Mark's Gospel were written out somewhat as follows:

THBEGINNINGOTHGOSPELOJESUSXTTHESONOGOD

There was practically no punctuation and there was no verse numbering nor chapter divisions. The book itself was a large one kept in church. It is no wonder that writers did not always check their quotations from Scripture but relied upon their memories. Nor is it surprising that notes tended to get written in the margin; and that sometimes notes were transferred by copyists to the body of the text. When cursive writing became common, the more difficult uncial manuscripts became neglected. We may be grateful that so many of them have survived destruction by barbarian warriors and the normal processes of decay to be available for the correction of the biblical text to-day.

Vaticanus (B) is made from particularly fine parchment, said to have been prepared from antelope skins. It originally contained the whole Greek Bible; but of the approximately 820 original leaves only 759 remain. It has lost the beginning, up to Genesis 46.28. It has lost Psalms 106 to 138; some chapters from Hebrews, the Pastoral Epistles and the Revelation. As the late Sir Frederic Kenyon pointed out, though there is no exciting story of its finding, there is a lively enough story of the endeavours of scholars of many successive generations to overcome the obstacles which the officials of the Vatican Library for so long put in the way of its being studied.

A correspondent of Erasmus in 1533 sent that scholar a number of selected readings from it, as proof of its superiority to the received Greek text. In 1669 a collation (or statement of its various readings) was made by Bartolocci, but it was never published, and remained unknown until 1819. Other imperfect collations were made about 1720 and 1780. Napoleon carried the manuscript off as a prize of victory to Paris, where it remained till 1815, when the many treasures of which he had despoiled the libraries of the Continent were returned to their respective owners. While at Paris it was studied by Hug, and its great age and supreme importance were first fully made known; but after its return to Rome a period of seclusion set in. In 1843 Tischendorf, after waiting for several months, was allowed to see it for six hours. Next year De Muralt was permitted to study it for nine hours. In 1845 the great English scholar Tregelles was allowed indeed to see it but not to copy a word.

The Roman authorities themselves produced editions in 1857 and 1859, which were, however, full of inaccuracies. The indefatigable Tischendorf (we shall hear more of him) kept at it: though he broke the rules by copying out twenty pages instead of merely collating difficult passages; and his access was consequently restricted. However the result of his visits on only fourteen days, lasting only three hours each, enabled him to produce in 1867 the most accurate edition which had yet appeared. A better Roman edition began to come out in the following year: and in 1889–90 'a complete photographic facsimile of the whole MS. made its contents once and for all the common property of all scholars.'[1]

Of these great vellum codices *Vaticanus* is probably the earliest. It undoubtedly comes from the Fourth Century. In their edition of the Greek New Testament the English scholars Westcott and Hort gave special importance to *Vaticanus* and *Sinaiticus*, so that it has come to have a notable influence upon our Revised Version. More recent scholarship, supported by more recent discoveries, has denied this pre-eminence, and the existence of a so-called 'neutral text' which Westcott and Hort derived from it. But *Vaticanus* remains very important indeed.

The history of *Codex Sinaiticus* in modern times is an exciting one. In May 1844 the German scholar Tischendorf was travelling in search of manuscripts and arrived at the lonely monastery of St. Catherine, walled like a Norman castle, on the side of Mount Sinai. Here a large waste-paper basket caught his eye. The monk in charge of the library said that it contained old rubbish that would shortly be burned: two basketfuls had already been destroyed in this way. Tischendorf asked to see what it contained, and was amazed to find 129 leaves from what seemed to be the oldest Bible he had ever seen. It was from the Old Testament in Greek. Could he have this rubbish? Unfortunately Tischendorf does not appear to have possessed the advantage of

[1] *Our Bible and the Ancient Manuscripts*, pp. 138, 139.

PLATE III

St. Catherine's Monastery on Mount Sinai

what is called a 'poker face'. The monks could tell he was excited by his find. They let him have a third only. Later Tischendorf presented these forty-three leaves to Frederick Augustus II of Saxony. They are still in the Library of the University of Leipzig. In the king's honour they were named the *Codex Friderico-Augustanus*. Tischendorf published his find, correctly attributing it to the middle of the Fourth Century A.D. But he did not say where he had found it. He did not want any scholars to get to Sinai before him.

Tischendorf was a poor man, who did not easily find means for travel. Also there were other claims of scholarship. In 1850 he produced his edition of the *Codex Amiatinus*; in 1852 of the *Codex Claromontanus*. In 1853 he was able to travel to the East again. This time the monks of Sinai proved unhelpful. All he got hold of was a fragment containing a few verses of Genesis. In 1859 he was back again.

This time he was cautious. He talked about anything and everything except biblical manuscripts. On the last night he mentioned them casually in a conversation with the monastery steward. 'The latter, anxious to display his own learning, remarked "And I, too, have a Septuagint", that is, the Greek Old Testament; and so saying he took down from a shelf over the door of his cell a bulky parcel wrapped in a red cloth, which he untied, revealing to Tischendorf's astonished gaze not merely the leaves which he had rescued from the flames fifteen years before, but other parts of the Old Testament, and the New Testament complete, with two early Christian works, the Epistle of Barnabas and the "Shepherd" of Hermas. Tischendorf casually asked, and readily obtained, permission to borrow the volume for the night; and, alone in his cell, he set to work to copy the Epistle of Barnabas, the original Greek text of which had been known only in very imperfect copies.'[1]

Tischendorf persuaded the monks to send the manuscript to Cairo, where there was a branch of the monastery. There he spent two months in copying it. But this was not

[1] *The Codex Sinaiticus & The Codex Alexandrinus*, p. 6.

really satisfactory. How could he persuade them to give it up? At last the idea occurred to him to persuade them to present it to the Tsar of Russia, who was patron of his travels; and also the traditional protector of the Eastern Orthodox Churches. The project attracted the monks. The Archbishopric of Sinai had fallen vacant. It would be useful to gain the Tsar's support for their nominee: moreover it was natural to expect that if they presented this volume to the Tsar they would, like the deacons who transported the loads of Bibles to Constantine in the Fourth Century, experience the Emperor's liberality. The negotiations were long and involved. In 1862 Tischendorf published a version of the codex in facsimile type; but it was not until 1867 that the codex was presented to the Tsar and placed in the Imperial Public Library at St. Petersburg. In return the monks of St. Catherine received 9,000 roubles—then worth £1,350—and a number of Russian decorations. Their nominee had also secured the coveted Archbishopric. The monks of the period were satisfied with the bargain and remained friendly to Tischendorf: some of their successors have resented it and sought to traduce his memory.

Originally *Codex Sinaiticus* must have contained about 730 leaves. Only 390 exist to-day: 242 in the Old Testament and 148 in the New. Forty-three of the leaves are in Leipzig: the rest are in the British Museum. The New Testament section is complete and contains also the so-called Epistle of Barnabas, which was at some times and places included in the Scriptures. Early fathers regarded it as genuine; but by the time that *Sinaiticus* was written this was largely disbelieved and it is a little surprising to find it in this manuscript. It is an early work, inspired by an anti-Jewish passion, written to prevent Christians from returning to Judaism. There is also in the manuscript a part of the 'Shepherd' of Hermas, another popular early writing which for a time had its place in Scripture. It is possible that other books existed at the end of the original manuscript.

Work upon the text has revealed some interesting facts. The writing is the work of three different scribes. One wrote out most of the historical and poetical books of the Old Testament as well as most of the New Testament and the Epistle of Barnabas. A second wrote the Prophets and the 'Shepherd' of Hermas. A third wrote the whole of Tobit and Judith, the first half of 4 Maccabees and the first two-thirds of the Psalms. In the New Testament he re-wrote six pages, perhaps to correct mistakes. The first scribe was a poor speller; the second betrays an illiteracy which is 'so startling that it is indeed a puzzle to understand how he can ever have been chosen to work on a manuscript of this sort.'[1] The spelling of the third scribe is, however, exemplary.

This bad spelling has made it clear that the manuscript was written from dictation. Perhaps the narrow columns recall the papyrus rolls from which the copy was taken. At one point the reader must have had before him indecipherable numeral. It is in 1 Maccabees 5.20 where other manuscripts read '8,000'. The dictator read out 'either six or three thousand' and 'either six or three thousand' it remains.

The monks of St. Catherine in the Nineteenth Century may not have thought much of the old manuscript, which was almost miraculously saved from destruction. That it was greatly valued much earlier is evidenced by the great number of corrections it contains. Tischendorf counted 14,800 of these; and his enumeration did not include the pages of the manuscript which he had secured for Leipzig. Most of these corrections are of tiny points or of minor significance: in the Gospels, however, they are particularly numerous, and sometimes of real importance. In Matthew 6.28 *Sinaiticus* has the unique reading that the lilies of the field 'neither card nor spin': an early corrector has changed it to the usual reading. In Matthew 17.21 the words 'Howbeit this kind goeth not out but by prayer and fasting' are

---

[1] *Ibid.*, p. 15.

omitted: an early corrector has supplied their lack. Many of these corrections are indeed very early. Some have been supplied by the scribes themselves as they went over their work. It is possible that, in a number of instances, both text and variant were actually copied from the manuscript which the scribe—or rather the man to whose dictation the scribe was working—had before him. All this sets problems for the textual critics of to-day.

How can we tell the date of this codex? We are dependent almost entirely upon the evidence of the handwriting. Anyone who has had anything to do with old registers knows that there is an obvious difference between the handwriting of the Seventeenth Century and the Nineteenth; that there is often a discernible difference between the handwriting of the Nineteenth Century and the Twentieth. Yet it is not wise to dogmatize upon periods which are close to one another: there are people still alive who write with the clear penmanship which they acquired—perhaps in some village school—sixty and more years ago. Differences can also be detected—often quite easily—between the style of writing common in England, France and the U.S.A. Readers of detective stories know how important the evidence of handwriting often is. The scholars who have brought detective work on ancient manuscripts to a fine art, and to something very near an exact science, are known as palæographers. Their researches become more important the further back we press in the history of the written Bible. They are quite sure that *Codex Sinaiticus* cannot have been written later than the Fourth Century. Many of them are fairly confident that it best be dated in the first half of that century.

At the same time other evidence shows that the book cannot be dated earlier than the Fourth Century. The text of the Gospels has been divided up into numbered sections upon a plan devised by Eusebius of Caesarea, who lived from 265 to 340. It is extremely unlikely that this could have been adopted before A.D. 300. The new enumeration has been inserted by the scribes themselves: it is clear that it

PLATE IV

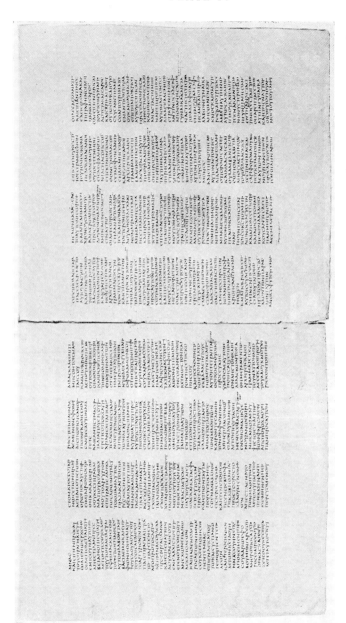

Codex Sinaiticus
(St. Luke 19.13–20.34)

was contemporary with them. This makes it all the more likely that it is to be dated around A.D. 350.

Vellum was expensive and not always easily obtainable. It must have required quite a flock of sheep to provide the skins for *Codex Sinaiticus*; and if *Vaticanus* is indeed made of antelope skins it represents the spoil of a considerable hunting party. Vellum was also extremely durable. In the Middle Ages, when a monastery required some new book, there might not be the necessary skins available in the scriptorium. So many a scribe decided to 'make do and mend.' Just as an amateur painter in oils buys old canvases to cover with his fresh attempts, so the monastic librarian would look through his shelves to find a volume, which no one had recently consulted, which might be used again. Perhaps a new Bible had recently been made or acquired. Why not use an old one for the new book? Water and a scrubbing brush would be produced to clean the skins for fresh use. Fortunately medieval detergents were not always very effective. With a number of these volumes it has proved possible to make sense of the original writing; and some of these palimpsests, as they are called, are very valuable.

One of the most important biblical manuscripts is a palimpsest. This is a volume in the National Library of Paris, called the *Codex Ephraemi*, or C. It was brought to Italy early in the Sixteenth Century from the East and then taken to France by Catherine de Medici. On the face of it, it is a book containing thirty-eight treatises in Syriac, written by St. Ephraim, the Syrian Father (d. 373). The copy was made in Egypt in the Twelfth Century. But scholars came to realise that far greater interest attached to the earlier writing—which was obviously biblical—which lay beneath it. The English scholar Bentley instigated work upon it early in the Eighteenth Century. But no great success was achieved until Tischendorf reached Paris more than a century later. He produced an edition of the New Testament in this version in 1843 and of the Old Testament in 1845.

Unfortunately the whole Bible is not available. The original codex was hacked about for the making of the new book in the Twelfth Century. It came originally from a complete Bible. Sixty-four leaves are left of the Old Testament, containing parts of Job, Proverbs, Ecclesiastes, Wisdom, Ecclesiasticus and the Song of Solomon. There are a hundred and forty-five New Testament leaves, out of an original two hundred and thirty-eight, containing portions of every book except 2 Thessalonians and 2 John. The Gospels are divided up into sections on the lines of Eusebius: and from the writing it is believed that the original codex was written in the Fifth Century, a little later than *Alexandrinus*. The text has affinities with that of the Syriac versions, which gives an indication of the area where it originated.

In this chapter we have had opportunity to deal only with some of the most famous uncial manuscripts. There are many more, the pride of libraries in the old world and in the new. When one considers the treatment which books have suffered from, the hazards they have had to face, the marvel is not that so few manuscripts exist as that there are so many; and that the work of scholars has done so much to bring their meaning and significance to light.

Chapter Eight

THE EARLIEST GREEK MANUSCRIPTS

IN THE century before the making of the great codices which we have been considering Bible reading was a normal accompaniment of Christian life. Churches owned Bibles, or parts of them—and if one owned a complete Bible it would be in several parts—and so did an increasing number of private individuals. The tolerant Clement of Alexandria (died *c.* A.D. 220) is often contrasted with Tertullian, the puritan controversialist from North Africa (A.D. 160 to 230). Clement regarded philosophy as 'a "schoolmaster" to bring the Greek mind to Christ, as the Law brought the Hebrews.' Tertullian asked 'What is there in common between Athens and Jerusalem? What between heretics and Christians? . . . After Christ we desire no subtle theories.'[1] Yet both were agreed that married people should read the Scriptures together—that is to say, read them aloud to one another. Clement suggested that the best time for this was *before* the chief meal of the day—a sufficient indication to a modern family that it was a comparatively leisured class of readers that he had in mind.[2]

Yet the poor also had the Scriptures read to them. From an epistle, *De Virginitate*, which was falsely attributed to Clement, we learn of cottage-meetings, at which wealthier members of the Church, who owned books of the Bible, brought them for reading aloud.[3] In a Christian family the Scriptures were the basis of education. Origen (*c.* A.D. 185 to 254) recalled how during his boyhood the Bible was read daily and the children were set to learn passages by heart. We are reminded of the high estimation in which the books

[1] See Henry Bettenson, *Documents of the Christian Church* (Oxford, World's Classics, 1943), pp. 8 & 9.
[2] See Adolf Harnack, *Bible Reading in the Early Church* (London, 1912), p. 55.
[3] *Ibid.*, p. 63.

7

of the Apocrypha were held by his maintaining that young people should begin with easier books such as Esther, Judith, Tobit and Wisdom, before going on to the Psalms, the Gospels and the Epistles. Then, as now, much of the language of the Psalms would be picked up by joining in public worship. Eusebius (c. A.D. 265 to 340) indeed mentions that it was usual for children to begin by learning the Bible canticles.[1]

Learning by heart played a great part in the ancient world—a fact which has to be remembered when we consider the educational work of the first Christian missionaries.[2] Ordinary Christians carried a good deal in their minds; and when writers made reference to the Bible they did so from memory, seldom with meticulous accuracy. And, as in the Middle Ages, there were some men whose memories were prodigious. Eusebius met in Palestine a blind Egyptian, who had been exiled from his country, of whom he wrote that 'he possessed whole books of the Holy Scriptures not on tables of stone, as the divine Apostle says, nor on skins of beasts or on papyrus, which moth and time can devour, but . . . in his heart, so that, as from a rich literary treasure, he could, ever as he wished, repeat now passages from the Law and the Prophets, now from the historical books, now from the Gospels and the Apostolic epistles.'[3] He sounds very like a Waldensian in the Middle Ages!

Irenaeus (c. A.D. 120 to 202) was another early Christian writer who inculcated Bible reading. 'Let a man take refuge in the Church,' he wrote, 'let him be educated in her bosom and be nourished from the Holy Scriptures. The Church is planted like Paradise in this world; of every tree of this Paradise shall ye eat; that is, eat ye from every Scripture of the Lord.'[4] He also makes it clear that in his time there was no lack of biblical manuscripts. For the

[1] *Ibid.*, p. 73.
[2] Cf. the present author's *A Fresh Approach to the New Testament* (London, 1950), pp. 94–96.
[3] Harnack, *op. cit.*, p. 83.
[4] *Ibid.*, p. 53 and n.

modern scholar early copies of the Revelation of St. John are rarer than of most other books. Yet Irenaeus had consulted numerous manuscripts of this particular book and paid particular attention to the older and more authentic copies.

Of the period between Irenaeus and Eusebius—which is that immediately before the great codices—Harnack concludes that 'the Pauline motto "Faith comes from preaching" was completed by the other, "Faith comes from reading". Neither did the Christians in their procedure pay too much attention to the warning of our Lord: "Give not that which is holy to the dogs, neither cast ye your pearls before swine"; they wished rather to do too much than too little. No doubt a powerful stimulus was thus given to the extension of the art of reading, and therein of education. The Church was compelled to lay stress upon Bible reading because, according to her doctrine, souls could be lost through *want of knowledge*, and so she became the great elementary school-master of the Greeks and the Romans. And not of these peoples only. The Church, especially the Greek Church—for the Latin Church proceeded otherwise —pressed on to translation of the Bible into other tongues, and by thus neglecting her own national prerogative laid the foundations of national literature among peoples that hitherto had possessed no literature, and in some cases were even without the knowledge of writing. All this came about because the Greeks demanded that the Bible must be read.'[1]

Yet, if this is true, why is it that modern knowledge of the Greek Bible has for so long found a full stop in the codices which were prepared at a rather later time, after the conversion of Constantine? In answer to this question there are four things to be said: (i) As we have already seen, large numbers of biblical manuscripts were destroyed in the persecution of Diocletian. (ii) Far earlier manuscript copies of the Scriptures are in existence than of the classics of

[1] *Ibid.*, pp. 85, 86.

Greece and Rome. (iii) The material upon which earlier scribes worked was not durable. As Eusebius pointed out, moth and time devoured them. (iv) Many recent discoveries of much earlier material have taken knowledge of the text back behind the famous codices.

In biblical times a tall plant called papyrus grew in thick clumps in the Nile valley. To-day, strangely enough, it is not found there at all, though it grows in other parts of North Africa and in Sicily. To the people of Egypt this plant was almost as valuable as the bamboo has been to the Chinese. It was used for building, for boats, for mats, and for many household needs. The ark in which the infant Moses was hidden among the reeds was made of papyrus stalks, caulked with bitumen and pitch. Isaiah 18.2 has a reference to ambassadors who descended the Nile in vessels of papyrus; and in Job 9.26 there is a reference to the great speed of these ships of reed. For our purpose, however, the importance of the plant is that from its pith there was produced a writing substance which was widely used. It is very like paper and it is from the word *papyrus* that our word paper is derived: the Greek word for the pith was *biblos*, and from it comes bible. A considerable trade was done in papyrus sheets, and in the rolls which could be made by fastening the sheets together. It was exported from Egypt and there were shops for its sale in Rome, where it became a carefully graded merchandise. Originally the best quality was called *hieratica* (for sacred use) but in the First Century A.D. flatterers re-named the best after the Emperor Augustus, the second-best after his wife, Livia—and it was only the third-best that was called hieratica.

Strips of the pith were scraped from the stalks of the plant, wetted, and laid flat in parallel lines: a second set was laid on top across them. They were pressed together with Nile water (where this was used, glue was hardly needed) and when the sheets were dried they were smoothed out ready for the pen. It was naturally more convenient to use the side in which the strips were laid horizontally. This is called the *recto*. But the other side, or *verso*, might come in useful later on. 'Official documents in particular which were no longer required were frequently utilized for other purposes, the original writing being either crossed out or washed out, as when we find a private letter written over an official notice of a death, or as when the *verso* of an old taxing-list serves a schoolmaster and his pupil for a writing-lesson.'[1]

The material was comparatively tough; but obviously it was not made to last. It was particularly susceptible to damp; and, when it did not become damp, it became in time very brittle. The dry climate of Egypt, however, and its sandy soil, which quickly covered over accumulations of 'waste-paper' dumped outside a town, provided the necessary protective conditions for the preservation of papyri. From Egypt, partly from tombs, partly from the wrappings of crocodile-mummies, but mostly from rubbish-heaps, there has been brought out a quantity of material which, in the past sixty years, has brought much illumination to New Testament studies.

Scholars were slow in appreciating the significance of what was being unearthed. In 1863 Bishop Lightfoot remarked of a New Testament word which had only been found previously among classical writers in Herodotus, more than five hundred years earlier: 'You are not to suppose that the word had fallen out of use in the interval, only that it had not been used in the books which remain to us: probably it had been part of the common speech all along. I will go further, and say that if we could only recover letters that ordinary people wrote to each other without any thought of being literary, we should have the greatest possible help for the understanding of the language of the New Testament generally.'[2]

---

[1] George Milligan, *Selections from the Greek Papyri* (Cambridge, 1910), Introduction, p. xxii.
[2] H. H. Moulton, *A Grammar of New Testament Greek*, Vol. i, *Prolegomena*, 3rd edition (Edinburgh, 1908), p. 242.

That recovery has been made. The materials for it were already accumulating while Lightfoot spoke. It has indeed provided 'the greatest possible help for the understanding of the New Testament.' Unfortunately the student who took down Lightfoot's words did not record the actual word of which he was speaking, so we do not know whether it has actually been illuminated by discoveries among the papyri or not.[1] Many words and phrases have, however, gained a fresh significance. Thus we know now that when Jesus forbade his disciples to carry a scrip (Mark 6.8) He had in mind the kind of begging-bag which wandering preachers might be expected to take with them; that when the younger son in the parable 'gathered all together' (Luke 15.13, A.V.) what he did was to realize his assets, converting them into ready cash. In Colossians 2.14, where St. Paul wrote of *blotting out* the handwriting of ordinances he was using the verb employed for process of cleansing a papyrus sheet so that it might be used again.

This knowledge has come from a study of 'the wills, official reports, private letters, petitions, accounts, and other trivial survivals from the rubbish-heaps of antiquity.'[2] The papyri date from four centuries before Christ to four centuries after, and later. What has been found through their study is that the writers of the New Testament were using what was very nearly the common Greek which, since the conquests of Alexander the Great, was so widely diffused as a second language throughout the Near East. Very nearly: but not quite. The writers of the New Testament had been brought up on the Old Testament; and this affected their writings more, probably, than the first enthusiasts for the new knowledge were ready to admit.

Not only does a study of the papyri illuminate words and phrases: it shows that in the letters written by St. Paul which we know as the Epistles in the New Testament, the evangelist was using the ordinary letter form of the time,

---

[1] See C. F. D. Moule, *The Language of the New Testament* (inaugural lecture, Cambridge, 1952), p. 5.

[2] Moulton, *op. cit.*, p. 3.

and transforming it. An ordinary letter, from one ordinary pagan to another, would follow this order:

> Opening address or salutations.
> Thanksgiving and prayer for the one addressed.
> The substance of the letter.
> Farewell greetings and closing prayer.[1]

It will at once be realised that the pattern is familiar to the New Testament reader. Paul varied the formula with a delightful freedom. Where at the beginning the reader would expect the word *chairein*, meaning 'greetings' he put instead *charis*, which means 'grace'.

Papyri appear first to have come onto the market in 1778, when some Egyptian peasants produced a chest containing about fifty specimens. But there were no buyers. The peasants burned the papyri—for the sake of the pleasant smell which they gave out: only one was rescued, and is now in the Museum at Naples. In the early years of the Nineteenth Century other papyri were brought to the West. They attracted little attention at first. From 1877 onwards, however, work upon them was continuous. Two Oxford scholars, B. P. Grenfell and A. S. Hunt, were among the foremost. The German scholar Adolf Deissmann wrote *Light from the Ancient East*, an epoch-making book. And in this country J. H. Moulton and G. Milligan began, and Milligan completed, a *Vocabulary of the Greek New Testament Illustrated from the Papyri and Other Non-literary Sources*, which has become a necessary tool for all serious New Testament students.

This new knowledge has been derived from non-literary sources, not from carefully constructed books written in an academic style, but from what was intended to be ephemeral, casual correspondence, inexact in punctuation and spelling, day to day business records, invitations to dinner, contracts of different kinds—just the sort of material which in modern Britain, in a time of paper shortage, is collected to be pulped.

[1] See *Light from Ancient Letters*, by Henry G. Meecham (London, 1923), ch. 5.

Christian scholars have naturally been on the look-out for anything which bears the name of Christ: and Milligan's little text-book of *Selections from the Greek Papyri*[1] contains in its fifty-five specimens two early Christian letters, a Christian prayer, and a Christian amulet, meant, like a heathen amulet, to be worn round the neck. The fact that this had been worn in this way meant that the papyrus roll had been closely pressed together. This made it very difficult to decipher; but in the end it was discovered to be a prayer for health, leading into the Lord's Prayer.

Great excitement was caused when Grenfell and Hunt reported that in their excavations of the site of Oxyrhynchus, a hundred and twenty miles south of Cairo, on the edge of the Libyan desert, they had found a single leaf from a papyrus book, containing Sayings of Jesus, some of which were quite unknown. These were published in 1897. A later visit produced a second sheet of sayings (though not from the same book) and some fragments of a lost Gospel. These were published in 1904.

Papyri are mostly fragmentary. In the text which has been preserved there are often edges broken off, or holes in the middle. The editor's task is not merely to estimate from the handwriting the date of the manuscript and write it out afresh in Greek characters for printing. Before he can make a translation he has to conjecture what word or words may have been written in the missing space—which calls for a nice sense both of sympathetic invention and ruthless discrimination. When the sayings discovered in 1897 were first published the translation of the most interesting of them read: 'Jesus saith, Wherever there are . . . and there is one . . . alone, I am with him. Raise the stone and there thou shalt find me, cleave the wood and there am I.'[2] In a later edition the suggested translation of the opening sentence read, 'Wherever there are (two) they are not without God, and wherever there is one alone, I say, I am

[1] (Cambridge, 1910) pp. 125–134.
[2] *Sayings of Our Lord*, published for the Egypt Exploration Fund by Henry Frowde (London, 1897), p. 12.

with him.' The manuscript of these sayings is thought to have come from the early Third Century. The second discovery was of a rather later date, but not later than A.D. 300. The first saying among these is perhaps the most interesting: 'Jesus saith, Let not him who seeks . . . cease until he finds, and when he finds he shall be astonished; astonished he shall reach the kingdom, and having reached the kingdom he shall rest.'[1]

These discoveries substantiated the belief, already widely held by scholars, that collections of the sayings of Jesus had existed in early days alongside the fuller setting forth of the deeds and teaching of Jesus which we call Gospels. Were there any other Gospels also? Certainly there were plenty later on, romantic inventions of a wonder-loving age, which bear such titles as the Gospel of Thomas, the Gospel of Bartholomew, the Gospel according to the Egyptians, the Gospel of the Infancy.[2] It has been well said that these were not excluded from the New Testament: they excluded themselves. But were there any genuine gospels as well as Matthew, Mark, Luke and John?

Certainly the chosen four established their primacy early: for the Church historian, Irenaeus, writing in the Second Century, could dogmatize as follows:

It is impossible that the Gospels should be in number either more or fewer than these. For since there are four regions of the world wherein we are, and four principal winds, and the Church is as seed sown in the whole earth, and the Gospel is the Church's pillar and ground, and the breath of life: it is natural that it should have four pillars, from all corners breathing incorruption, and kindling men into life. Whereby it is evident, that the Artificer of all things, the Word, who sitteth upon the Cherubim, and keepeth all together, when He was made manifest unto men, gave us His Gospel in four forms.

[1] *New Sayings of Jesus and Fragment of a Lost Gospel* (Egypt Exploration Fund, 1904), p. 13. This also contains the revised translation of the sayings discovered earlier.
[2] See M. R. James, *The Apocryphal New Testament* (Oxford, 1924).

The argument is not very convincing; but Irenaeus' very certainty is an indication that not many of his readers can have heard of more than four Gospels. Were there any more?

There is a little evidence that there were. Some might be local Gospels, with a very limited circulation. In 1904 Grenfell and Hunt published a small fragment of a few verses, mostly parallel with the Sermon on the Mount. But there is, in addition, a question from the disciples, 'When wilt thou be manifest to us, and when shall we see thee?' to which Jesus answered, 'When ye shall be stripped and not ashamed' —which is similar to a passage in the apocryphal Gospel according to the Egyptians. The few verses available are not enough for a judgment to be made: but they appear to come from a Gospel which has affinities rather with the first three, or Synoptic, Gospels, than with the Gospel of John.

In the Summer of 1934 the authorities of the British Museum purchased from a dealer a collection of papyri from Egypt. Among them were fragments, which the evidence of handwriting assigned to the middle of the Second Century, which quite clearly contained portions of an unknown Gospel. This was probably a copy of a Gospel already in circulation, not the author's manuscript: and, if so, the book itself was likely to have been written not later than the period A.D. 110–130, that is to say, just before the period when the Four Gospels we know so well displaced all others. What is particularly interesting is that the fragments in some ways resemble more nearly in style the Fourth Gospel than the Synoptics. The longest of the fragments has been translated as follows. Words which are missing in the Greek and have been conjecturally restored are enclosed in square brackets, with a question-mark where there is serious doubt about correctness of restoration. This small sample will give a fair idea of the work which palæographical scholars have to do in making the results of these discoveries available for biblical students:

PLATE V

Verso

Recto

A Fragment of an Unknown Gospel

. . . com]ing unto him began to tempt him with a qu[estion], s[aying], Master Jesus, we know that thou art come [from God], for the things which thou doest te[stify] above all the prophets. [Tell] us [therefore]: Is it lawful [?to rend]er unto kings those things which pertain unto their rule? [Shall we] r[ender(?) unto th]em, or n[ot]? But Jesus, knowing [thei]r [th]ought, being moved with indig[nation], said [unto] t[hem], Why call ye me with yo[ur mou]th [M]aster, when ye [hea]r n[ot] what I [s]ay? Well did I[saiah] p[ro]phesy [of yo]u, saying, [Thi]s [people honour] me with the[ir li]ps, [but] their [hear]t [is fa]r from m[e. I]n vain [do they worship me, teaching as their doctrines the] prece[pts of men . . .[1]

We have discussed the importance of the discoveries of papyrus 'rubbish' in Egypt and their importance for our understanding of the New Testament. We have seen that some scraps of unknown Gospels have also been found. But, it may well be asked, what about the canonical Gospels, copies of which must have been far more numerous? Have no fragments been found of the biblical manuscripts which Churches and private people owned in the age before Constantine? As early as 1836 the British Museum secured thirty-two leaves of the Psalms in Greek: but these were very late papyri, from the Seventh Century. During their time on the site of Oxyrhynchus in 1896 and 1897 Grenfell and Hunt found, in addition to the page of sayings of Jesus, a folded sheet from a codex of St. John. The original book must have contained about twenty-five of these folded sheets; and this is the outermost but one. It contains John 1: 23–31 and 33–41 on the first leaf, and on the second, John 20: 11–17 and 19–25. Particular interest attaches to this find, because it was formerly thought that the codex form was not employed before vellum came into use: but

---

[1] *The New Gospel Fragments* (British Museum, 1951), p. 13. See also the fuller *Fragments of an Unknown Gospel and Other Early Christian Papyri* (British Museum, 1935).

this sheet is from a *papyrus* codex. Its date is Third Century. So we are back before Constantine.

In 1927 two other publications claimed the interest of scholars. In Washington there were issued the Freer Greek MS. V, which contained portions of thirty-three leaves of a codex of the Minor Prophets, which comes probably from the latter part of the Third Century. This gives a text from Amos 1.10 to the end of Malachi (with most of Hosea missing) which is a hundred years earlier than *Codex Vaticanus*. A mutilated codex of Genesis 1.16–35.8 was issued in Berlin. Its importance is again that it takes us back behind *Codex Vaticanus*, which has been the normal authority for the Greek Old Testament. In 1936 the John Rylands Library at Manchester published a tiny scrap of Deuteronomy, which is believed to be from the Second Century B.C., and thus the oldest portion of the Greek Old Testament now known to scholars. These and other finds are of less importance, however, than that which was first announced in 1931, a discovery comparable in importance to the finding of *Codex Sinaiticus*.

On November 17th of that year Sir Frederic Kenyon announced in *The Times* the discovery of twelve manuscripts—said to have been found in a Coptic graveyard, stowed away in jars—eight containing books of the Old Testament, three of the New, one containing parts of the apocryphal Book of Enoch and a Christian homily. These manuscripts were sold by dealers—who, by now, were well aware of the value of such things. The greater part of the find was purchased by Mr. A. Chester Beatty, an American living in England, and some was secured by the University of Michigan.

What had been found was probably the remnants of an early Christian library. The Old Testament include substantial portions of Genesis, which are largely missing from *Codex Vaticanus* and *Codex Alexandrinus*: and they are about a century older. Some portions of Numbers and Deuteronomy may belong to the first half of the Second Century. There are also fragments of Isaiah and Jeremiah, and the imperfect leaves of a codex containing the books of Ezekiel, Daniel and Esther. The Ezekiel leaves have become separated. Some are in the Chester Beatty while others are at Princeton University.

The New Testament books are more important still. One was originally a papyrus codex of the four Gospels and the Books of Acts. It is believed to have been written in the first half of the Third Century. There were originally one hundred and ten leaves, of which thirty remain. A second manuscript contained ten leaves from a codex of the Pauline epistles; but there were thirty more from the same book in the portions of the find acquired by the University of Michigan. Then Mr. Beatty obtained forty-six more leaves; so that there is now available an almost complete codex of the Epistles of St. Paul, which may date from as early as about A.D. 200. The Pastoral Epistles do not appear ever to have been in this volume; but it is interesting that Hebrews finds a place in it, immediately after Romans. A third New Testament manuscript contains about a third of the Book of Revelation, and probably comes from the second half of the Third Century.

The John Rylands Library in Manchester is one of those which have made collections of papyri. A catalogue of these was being prepared by Professor B. P. Grenfell. Subsequently the work devolved upon his collaborator, A. S. Hunt, and, upon his death in 1934, it was taken up by Mr. C. H. Roberts, University Student in Papyrology at Oxford. While he was sorting a group of papyri which had been acquired in Egypt by Professor Grenfell in 1920 he found a tiny scrap containing verses from St. John. On the *recto* there are parts of verses thirty-one to thirty-three and on the *verso* parts of verses thirty-seven and thirty-eight of the eighteenth chapter. His expert knowledge led him quickly to realise that he held in his hand the oldest fragment of the New Testament in the world.

The evidence of dating is, as we have seen, derived from

the style of handwriting. The distinctive character of this particular hand is described by Mr. Roberts as follows: 'The scribe writes in a heavy, rounded and rather elaborate hand, often uses several strokes to form a single letter (*cf.* the eta and particularly the sigma in Recto, l.3) with a rather clumsy effect and is fond of adding a small flourish or hook to the end of his strokes (*cf.* the omega, the iota and the upsilon); among particular letters the epsilon with its cross stroke a little above the centre, the delta, the upsilon and the mu may be noted.'[1] The next thing he had to do was to examine other manuscripts which displayed these characteristics. Were any of these dated? One was dated A.D. 94, another A.D. 127, another A.D. 117. Some of the peculiarities of the writing are also to be found in one dated A.D. 153. Other undated manuscripts of a similar type are assigned to the first half of the Second Century. It is to this period that this document has therefore been assigned: and is probably more likely to date from the first quarter of the Century than the second.

It is of interest that this earliest fragment of the New Testament comes from one of its later books. Indeed there have been writers who have dismissed St. John's Gospel as a late Second Century romance! This fragment probably came from Upper Egypt. The Fourth Gospel was probably written in Ephesus. It would have taken a good many years for a copy of what was written in Asia Minor to have reached Upper Egypt. Thus the evidence of this papyrus scrap helps to substantiate the belief, reached on quite other grounds, that the Fourth Gospel was written, not later than A.D. 100, and probably earlier. This little fragment is the nearest that we possess to the actual handwriting of the authors of the New Testament. The gap here may be only thirty or forty years.

[1] *An Unpublished Fragment of the Fourth Gospel* (Manchester University Press, 1935), p. 13.

PLATE VI

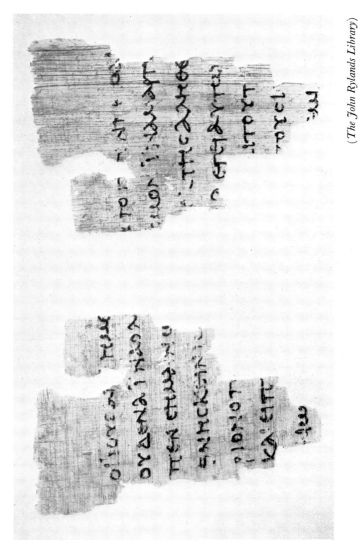

Verso

Recto

A Fragment of the Fourth Gospel

Chapter Nine

THE ORIGINS OF THE GREEK
OLD TESTAMENT

IN CHAPTER THREE we noticed that until recent years there had been available for scholars no manuscripts of the Hebrew Old Testament earlier than the Ninth Century A.D. Yet we have made reference all along to the Greek Old Testament, a translation from the Hebrew, and in the last two chapters we have seen that the great codices of the Fourth Century, and papyrus remains of an earlier date contained books or fragments of this Old Testament in Greek. It is as if there were translations of Chaucer into French hundreds of years earlier than any manuscripts of the English text! The Greek Old Testament was, indeed, the Bible of the early Church; and the Church succeeded in preserving it better than the Jews preserved the Hebrew from which it had been translated. How did this come about?

The history of the Fourth Century B.C. is dominated by Alexander of Macedon, one of the few figures of history named 'the great' who have truly deserved the title. His father Philip (382–336) had made a kingdom out of the congeries of Greek city-states: Alexander used the kingdom as springboard for a calculated plunge into the East, which won him an Empire. He defeated Persia, the traditional enemy of all Greek states, and took his conquests as far as India. From Samarcand to Cyrenaica all the world accepted Alexander as overlord. But his triumphs were short-lived as the conqueror himself. In 323, aged thirty-two years and eight months, Alexander died. His generals quarrelled over the division of his realms—for there was no heir to succeed him. One family, the Seleucids, became dominant in Syria: another, the Ptolemies, ruled Egypt. His influence remained. It was Alexander who made both necessary and possible a Greek version of the Old Testament.

In Egypt there had been founded the great city of Alexandria, one of many cities named after the conqueror. It became a great centre of Greek influence, a university centre second only to Athens. For the military conquests of Alexander had been accompanied by a more lasting cultural conquest. (Not that there was victory only on one side: the Greek spirit became a different thing through contact with the East; and many of Alexander's soldiers married Asiatic wives.) Wherever he went there went also Greek culture and the Greek language. All unknowing he was giving to the future Christian Church a most powerful means of propaganda and influence. Christianity arose in the Hellenistic Age—which might as accurately have been called the Alexandrine Age—the age in which the Greek language was dominant in commerce and culture and education. Words like *Abba*, *Epphatha* and *Talitha Cumi* remain in the Gospels to remind us that Jesus spoke Aramaic. There may be Aramaic or even Hebrew sources underlying the Gospels. But the whole New Testament was written in Greek. And the Old Testament which the New Testament quotes is, for the most part, the Greek Old Testament.

The Hebrew peoples had long been a shuttlecock driven to and fro by successive world powers, yet never wholly losing their individuality. In the Hellenistic Age there were many Jews in the valley of the Tigris: their Exile—the original historic Exile—has only ended in the last decade, with the expulsion of all Jews from the Kingdom of Iraq and their transport by aircraft to the State of Israel! There had been Jews in Egypt since the Sixth Century and their numbers were now greatly increasing. From a critical examination of the figures which have been handed down, the late Professor Lietzmann came to surprising conclusions. 'In both Egypt and Syria, there may well have been 1,000,000 Jews; in Palestine 500,000; in the rest of the Roman Empire at least 1,500,000. If there were 55,000,000 inhabitants in the Empire, at least 7 per cent of them must have been Jews', which was a far higher percentage than that in Germany in Nazi times. How this gigantic growth of Judaism had taken place remains, he wrote, an unsolved enigma; but he suggested that it might partly be accounted for by the absorption of other Semitic peoples.[1] It is not altogether surprising that some early chapters had already been written in the long and sorry story of anti-Semitism.

The first Ptolemy brought large numbers of Jewish and Samaritan captives to Alexandria, where many acquired civic rights. They were given a separate quarter of the city and their own ethnarch, who exercised judicial authority in all cases between Jew and Jew. The million Jews in Egypt in the Christian era constituted about an eighth of the population. At Leontopolis, for a time, a disused Egyptian temple was turned into a replica of the Temple at Jerusalem. It was more important that there were synagogues everywhere. They were attended by Greek-speaking Jews, who needed the Scriptures in their own language.

A process was inevitably taking place which has often been repeated in the modern world. The writer recalls contact with an Icelandic church in Western Canada, where the services were in Icelandic in the mornings and, in the evenings, mainly for the young people, in English. Children naturally acquire the language of their playmates and their schooling rather than the language of the 'old country' though it may still be used a good deal in the home. The second generation recalls the earlier speech as little more than a curiosity; and by the third generation it is forgotten. English is needed for business; for nine-tenths of the contacts of daily life. Similarly 'it was impossible for Jews who for generations spent their lives and carried on their business in Greek towns to retain their Semitic speech . . . In Alexandria a knowledge of Greek was not a mere luxury but a necessity of common life. If it was not required by the State as a condition of citizenship, yet self-interest

[1] *The Beginnings of the Christian Church* (2nd edition, London, 1949), p. 76.
8

compelled the inhabitants of a Greek capital to acquire the language of the markets and the Court. A generation or two may have sufficed to accustom the Alexandrian Jews to the use of the Greek tongue. . . . Every year of residence in Alexandria would increase their familiarity with Greek and weaken their hold upon the sacred tongue. Any prejudice which might have existed against the use of a foreign language would speedily disappear under a rule which secured full liberty in worship and faith. The adoption of the Greek tongue was a tribute gladly paid by the Alexandrian Jews to the great Gentile community which sheltered and cherished them.'[1]

The need for a Greek Bible was obvious. How was that need met? If we are to answer this question we must turn to an interesting Greek book called *The Letter of Aristeas*, in which the legend of the translation was set out, a legend accepted on its face value by the early Church and repeated with an increasing precision and elaboration of detail. The *Letter* purports to be written by a Greek Aristeas, who held high office at the court of Ptolemy Philadelphus (285–247 B.C.). Actually it belongs to a class of works which have been described as 'Jewish propaganda under a heathen mask.' Analysis reveals that it was written by a Jew, though one extremely familiar with the usages of the Alexandrian court, and at a later date than that of Philadelphus. It was natural, however, to link him with a story whose intention was to win Gentile interest for Hebrew learning, for he was a notable patron of scholarship, who had welcomed even a Buddhist mission to his court.[2] The *Letter* contains its own evidence of later construction—as when it alludes to the scrupulous care with which 'all business *used to be* transacted by these kings.' Recent study suggests that it was written between 150 and 100 B.C.,[3] more than a century after the events of which it purports to give a contemporary account.

[1] H. B. Swete, *An Introduction to the Old Testament in Greek* (Cambridge, 1900), pp. 8, 9.
[2] *Ibid.*, p. 16.
[3] Roberts, *op. cit.*, p. 103.

The story is that Demetrius of Phalerum, the royal librarian, was once asked by the king how many books there were in the library. 'More than two hundred thousand, O king', was the reply, 'and I will ere long make diligent search for the remainder, so that a total of half a million may be reached. I am informed that the Jews also have certain laws which are deserving of transcription and a place in the library.'

'What is to hinder thee then in this task?' replied the king. 'All the necessary means are at thy service.'

'Translation also is required', said Demetrius, 'for in the Jews' land they use a peculiar script and speak a peculiar language. It is commonly thought that they use the Aramaic language, but this is an error. It is another dialect.' When the king learned the facts he ordered that a letter should be sent to the high priest at Jerusalem to procure the necessary manuscripts and make possible a translation. The high priest was asked to send to Alexandria six elders learned in the law from each of the twelve tribes of Israel, to do the work. In time the seventy-two elders arrived bringing a copy of the Hebrew Law written in letters of gold on a roll composed of skins. On arrival they were given a banquet, at which they were tested by the king with difficult questions. Three days later they were taken by the librarian to the island of Pharos, where a building had been prepared for them. They set to work, comparing their results as they went on, and agreeing upon an approved version which Demetrius had copied. In seventy-two days the work was done.[1]

From this work of seventy-two elders in seventy-two days the word *Septuagint* was coined for this translation—not wholly accurately, for Septuagint means seventy and not seventy-two! It is often indicated by the abbreviation LXX. Later Christian legend declared that the translation was completed by the seventy-two, each in a separate cell,

[1] See *The Letter of Aristeas* (S.P.C.K. Translations of Early Documents, 1917), edited by H. St. J. Thackeray, M.A.

incommunicado, and that miraculously, when the final day
arrived, all the versions were found to be verbally identical.
What truth lies behind all this? That the LXX was produced
in Alexandria? Certainly: it bears all the marks of Alexandrian scholarship. That the translation was made by
visiting scholars from Jerusalem? The answer we have
made to the first question denies an affirmative answer to
the second. 'The LXX as a whole', wrote Swete, 'or at any
rate the earlier part of the collection, is a monument of
Alexandrian Greek as it was spoken by the Jewish colony in
the Delta under the rule of the Ptolemies.'[1] That the Hebrew
text was sent from Jerusalem? This seems more than likely,
though it would be surprising if it had indeed been written
in letters of gold.

It would be easy to say that the legend was invented to
explain the translation. But something else needs explanation too. The Jewish scholar Philo—roughly contemporary
with Jesus—recorded that down to his own day the completion of the LXX was celebrated by an annual festival at
Pharos. Swete points out that 'a popular anniversary of
this kind can scarcely have grown out of a literary work so
artificial and so wanting in the elements which ensure
popularity as the letter of Aristeas.'[2]

There we must leave it. But it is to be remembered that
the legend in the Letter refers only to the translation of the
Jewish Law, the first five books of the Old Testament, and
not the rest. Here again the tradition is certainly right in
stating that the Law came first. The complete LXX must
have been many years in the making. No doubt the section
of the Prophets (which included the main historical books)
came next, and that the third section of the Hebrew Bible,
known as the Writings, followed. The period in which the
translation was being made in Egypt was the same in which
the definite list of canonical books was being formed in
Palestine. No doubt as a book received its *imprimatur* in the

---

[1] *Op. cit.*, p. 21.
[2] *Ibid.*, p. 13.

home country a copy reached Alexandria to be translated and transcribed for circulation throughout the Dispersion. It is likely that by the beginning of the Christian era practically the whole of the Hebrew Scriptures were available in Alexandria in Greek.

We should remember that this was the first translation of the Bible into another language that was ever made. We take the idea of translation for granted: our own Christianity depends upon it. But there must have been many to whom the idea of using a foreign language for the sacred Scriptures, whose every syllable and letter was priceless beyond computation, must have appeared as blasphemy.

In the end the Septuagint was considerably larger than the Hebrew Bible. It contained the Book of the Wisdom of Solomon, a contemporary work of Alexandrian scholarship, in which the influence of Greek ideas is very apparent. It is a tempting suggestion that the optimism of Wisdom may be a reply to the pessimism of Ecclesiastes, whose place within the Hebrew canon has often occasioned surprise. It contained a Greek translation of the Hebrew Wisdom of Jesus the Son of Sirach, which is known to us by the title given in the Vulgate, Ecclesiasticus. It contained the historical Books of Maccabees, and a much longer version of Daniel —which included *The Song of the Three Holy Children*, in our Apocrypha (which Anglicans sing as the *Benedicite*) and the short detective story called *Bel and the Dragon*. Indeed it is roughly true to say that what we call the Apocrypha is made up of those books, or parts of books which are to be found in the Greek but not in the Hebrew Old Testament.[1] It was this enlarged Bible which became the Bible of the early Church, and we have seen how Origen held that religious education should begin with such books as Esther (which is also larger in the Greek version), Judith, Tobit and Wisdom.

[1] The exception is 2 Esdras, which is not found in any Greek manuscript, and comes to us from the Vulgate.

Was the LXX the first Greek Old Testament? 'The fact that quotations from a Greek version or versions still to be found in the New Testament and the works of Josephus and Philo, do not tally with the present Septuagint implies that there existed a number of early texts in Greek, and the problems raised by this fact are various and intricate.'[1] It is more likely, perhaps, that these quotations were made from more accurate versions of the LXX than we now possess. Yet probably there were fragmentary translations for the purpose of worship, produced early—just as Monsignor Knox issued his translation of the Epistles and Gospels before his version of the Bible. It is suggested also that parts of the Hebrew Bible were transliterated into Greek letters; so that the actual Hebrew words could be read aloud by those who would stumble over the letters of the Hebrew alphabet. This development is paralleled by the gradual abandonment, by large sections of the Orthodox Church, of the antique Cyrillic alphabet, maintained through the centuries for religious use, and the substitution of roman letters. The Germans, also, have largely given up their special form of gothic print, which was formerly used even for newspapers.

The Septuagint became very widely used; but its popularity among Christians brought in the end its abandonment and repudiation by Jews. The rendering, in Isaiah 7.14, of a Hebrew word, which normally means only young woman, by the Greek *parthenos* or virgin, played into the hands of Christian apologists, who found in Isaiah a prophecy of the virgin birth of Christ. The Jews determined to have nothing to do with anything that approached a free translation: the old spirit of exact reproduction must find a new dress. What they wanted was a translation word for word. This was provided for them by an ex-Christian, Aquila, in the Second Century A.D. The translator was a relative of the Emperor Hadrian, who employed him to supervise the building of the new city of Aelia Capitolina on the ruins of

---

[1] Roberts, *op. cit.*, p. 104.

Jerusalem. There he was converted to Christianity. But he soon found himself excommunicated because he would not abandon the pagan practice of astrology. He took his revenge upon a Church which would not accept upon his own terms so notable a convert by becoming a Jewish proselyte. He put himself to school under the best-known rabbis and learned Hebrew and much rabbinic lore. In time his version was accepted by Jews as more reliable than the Septuagint. The fragments which have been discovered show that it was indeed extremely literal, reproducing in Greek the peculiarities of Hebrew construction.

A later translator of the Old Testament into Greek was Theodotion. He was said, like Aquila, to have been a native of Pontus, and like him a proselyte from Christianity. It looks as if the two stories have got mixed up; and it is considered more likely that Theodotion was an Ephesian Jew. What he created was 'a free revision of the LXX rather than an independent translation.'[1] His version of Daniel was, however, almost invariably preferred to the Septuagint, so that there is hardly a manuscript in which it has not supplanted it. Another translator, Symmachus, appears to have written with Aquila's version before him, glancing aside now at Theodotion and now at the Septuagint. Yet 'again and again he goes his own way in absolute independence of earlier versions, and sometimes at least, it must be confessed, of the original.' He 'attempted to set himself free from the trammels of the Hebrew idiom and to clothe the thoughts of the Old Testament in the richer drapery of the Greek tongue.'[2]

Thus, by the Third Century A.D., there were four rival versions of the Greek Old Testament, the Septuagint, and the translations made by Aquila, Theodotion and Symmachus. The stage was set for the work of Origen (b. 185 or 186), a man remarkable enough in many fields of learning outside our immediate concern, but, for us, possessed

---

[1] Swete, *op. cit.*, p. 43.
[2] *Ibid.*, p. 52.

especially by remarkable critical gifts and astonishing industry. He deserves to be called the father of textual criticism, the predecessor of Erasmus and Ximenes and Stephanus, of Tischendorf and Westcott and Hort.

Origen was born of Christian parents in Alexandria. When he was only sixteen his father was martyred. By the age of eighteen he had become head of the catechetical school in Alexandria. From the first his interest was concentrated upon the Old Testament, and he took the unusual step, almost unprecedented for a Christian who was not of Jewish ancestry—of learning Hebrew. His life was spent between the two centres of Alexandria and Caesarea. It was to escape the persecution of Caracalla (216–219) that he went to Caesarea first. Then he returned to Egypt and his great period of literary activity began. In the next thirty years he produced commentaries or homilies on practically every book of the Old Testament. Controversy in Egypt drove him to Palestine again and his catechetical school at Caesarea became a centre of learning and a magnet for literary pilgrims.

What Origen chiefly sought was a really accurate text of the Greek Old Testament. He was disturbed by 'the great difference in the manuscripts, due either to the negligence of the scribes, or to the ill-advised daring of some in revising what is written, or even to those who add or omit in the revision whatever seems right to them.'[1] He thought that he could secure this by comparing the Greek with the Hebrew; for all the Hebrew manuscripts seemed to agree. What he did not know was that a similar process had taken place earlier in the Hebrew text; and that the Hebrew before him was not entirely the same as that from which the LXX was translated. He did not want to produce a new translation of his own. What he sought was the true Septuagint, which he revered as the Bible of the Church. Critical knowledge might lead him, for example, to reject

---

[1] Commentary on Matthew, quoted R. H. Pfeiffer, *Introduction to the Old Testament* (London, 1948), p. 108.

the Greek additions to the Book of Daniel; but, no, they were approved by the Church; to reject them in a fresh edition of the Septuagint would be to play into the hands of Jewish adversaries.

Scholars nowadays are accustomed to volumes in which different versions are set out in parallel columns. This method was evolved by Origen. He chose very short lines for each column, so that an exact comparison could be made. Twenty years' work lay behind the production of his tremendous *Hexapla*, or Sixfold version. In the first column he put the Hebrew text, in the second the Hebrew text transliterated into Greek characters. Third came the translation of Aquila, as nearest to the Hebrew, fourth that of Symmachus, as based upon Aquila, fifth the LXX, and sixth the translation of Theodotion, as based upon it. For some books other Greek texts, which he found, were added: these are known, from their position among the Greek columns, as the *Quinta*, *Sixta* and *Septima*. Later, also, he made a *Tetrapla*, or Fourfold version, omitting the first two Hebrew columns.

The transliteration of the Hebrew into Greek characters, in the few fragments which survive, is important to scholars because it suggests the way in which Hebrew was pronounced in Origen's time. The whole process of preparing the Hexapla was described by Eusebius and Jerome, who were full of admiration for Origen's tremendous industry. Much of the work was probably done by copyists, but it appears likely that the two Hebrew columns were written in Origen's own hand. Swete has calculated that 'the Hexapla, if written in the form of a codex, would have filled 3,250 leaves or 6,500 pages; and these figures are exclusive of the *Quinta* and *Sixta*, which may have swelled the total considerably. Even the *Tetrapla* would have exceeded two thousand leaves.'[1]

Nobody can have tried to copy this great work in its entirety; but it was kept in the library at Caesarea for

[1] *Op. cit.*, p. 74.

consultation. Here it was used by Jerome in the Fourth Century in the preparation of the Vulgate. Unfortunately, in 638, Caesarea was captured by the Saracens and nothing more was heard of the Christian library. Perhaps books were hidden, but none has ever come to light. 'Had the Hexapla been buried in Egypt, she might have preserved it in her sands; but it can scarcely be hoped that the sea-washed and storm-beaten ruins of Kaisaryeh cover a single leaf.'[1] Yet some fragments of copies of the famous six columns exist. The scholar who became Cardinal Mercati discovered at Milan in 1894 a palimpsest containing part of the Psalms, written in five of the six columns, the Hebrew being missing. The writing belongs to the Tenth Century A.D. The transliteration of the Hebrew into Greek characters is of great interest. In the Cambridge University Library—discovered in a way which will be described in the next chapter—there is a fragment containing part of Psalm 22 in all six columns.

Origen's work, we recall, was directed towards establishing a true text of the Septuagint. The results of a consideration of the other columns were noted in the fifth. He made a ruthless correction of the text in the light of the Hebrew which was available for him. But he made clear all the time what he was doing. He employed a number of signs which had already been evolved for correcting editions of Homer. Passages found in the LXX but not in the Hebrew he marked with an obelus (— or ÷ or ÷). Where the Hebrew contained passages which were not in the LXX he supplied these from the translation of Theodotion. The passage was marked by an asterisk (*) and its conclusion by a metobelus (: or /. or ·/.).

Unfortunately, however, most of Origen's admirers were more interested in results than in methods. After his death his disciples Pamphilus and Eusebius both issued editions of the Septuagint column alone. As copies were made the signs by which the additions and alterations were

[1] Swete, p. 75.

indicated came to be dropped. They had, indeed, little significance when the parallel columns were removed. The result was that Origen's version of the LXX became the standard one in many places, and that the great scholar who aimed at clarity only succeeded in making confusion worse confounded. 'Strictly speaking,' says Pfeiffer, 'the Septuagint is an unknown entity. It is uncritical to speak of the printed editions of the Greek text preserved in manuscripts as "the LXX", although this practice is well-nigh universal.'[1] Fortunately, however, just before the capture of Caesarea by the Saracens a Mesopotamian bishop made a translation of the fifth column of the Hexapla into Syriac, and an Eighth Century copy of this, reproducing faithfully all the critical signs, is in the Museum at Milan. It lacks the Pentateuch, but includes the Prophets as well as Job, Psalms, Proverbs, Ecclesiastes and the Song of Solomon.

Meanwhile other editors were at work on the Septuagint. Hesychius, who may be the Egyptian bishop of that name, who was martyred in 311, made corrections of the text. Jerome tells us that Church writers in Egypt made their quotations from the text of Hesychius, and it is from this source that fragments of the revision may be recovered. In Antioch another revision was associated with the name of Lucian, who was put to death for his faith a year later than Hesychius. Once again we are dependent upon quotations for recovery of the text. 'Our principal witness for Hesychius is Cyril of Alexandria (d. 444), while Chrysostom (d. 407) and Theodoret (d. c. 457) quoted Lucian.'[2] These independent attempts at clarification did not greatly help. In Jerome's time, 'men read their Old Testament in the recension of Lucian, if they lived in North Syria, Asia Minor, or Greece; in that of Hesychius, if they belonged to the Delta or the valley of the Nile; in Origen's Hexaplaric edition, if they were residents at Jerusalem or Caesarea.'[3]

[1] *Op. cit.*, p. 107.
[2] Pfeiffer, *op. cit.*, p. 111.
[3] Swete, *op. cit.*, p. 85.

In the light of all this, where do the great codices stand?
Most interesting is *Codex Sinaiticus* (ℵ), for a note by one
of its correctors states that it had been collated with a very
ancient manuscript which had been corrected by Pamphilus,
the successor and disciple of Origen, who had compared it
with the Hexapla itself. This means that the corrector of ℵ,
now in the British Museum, was only at a third remove
from Origen. The text of *Codex Alexandrinus* (A) is described
by the experts as Hexaplaric. Of *Vaticanus* the great Cambridge scholar, F. C. Burkitt, wrote more than forty years
ago that 'very few scholars have realised till lately the
terrible extent to which the text of B is disfigured by un-
skilful sporadic correction from the Hexapla.'[1] The text of
Codex Colberto-Sarravianus (G) which dates from the early
Fifth or late Fourth Century, is an important one for the
Septuagint. Its text is Hexaplaric, and it retains many of
the original critical signs, though these have not always
been accurately recorded. A hundred and fifty-three leaves
remain of this codex: one hundred and thirty are at
Leyden, twenty-two at Paris and one at Leningrad. *Codex
Basiliano-Vaticanus* (N) at Rome and *Codex Venetus* (V) at
Venice are now realised to be different parts of one codex,
written in the Eighth or Ninth Century. Its text is Lucianic.
A Ninth-Century *Codex Bodleianus* (I) at Oxford is important
because its margins contain readings from Aquila, Symmachus, and Theodotion, and from the *Quinta* and *Septima*
of the Hexapla.

The Chester Beatty discoveries have meant that 'the
darkness that hides the early history of the Septuagint has
been pushed back some two hundred years.'[2] These papyri
contain Old Testament texts, however, which are not very
greatly different from those of the vellum codices. The text of
the Freer Greek MS. V at Washington—portions of thirty-
three leaves of the Minor Prophets—'is free from Hexaplaric influences, but shows about thirty accommodations

---

[1] Quoted Roberts, *op. cit.*, p. 154.
[2] C. H. Roberts, *Two Biblical Papyri* (Manchester, 1936), p. 10.

with the Hebrew of its own.'[1] In the Rylands Library at Manchester there are some fragments of Deuteronomy, skilfully removed from the wrappings of a mummy. Their editor claims that 'we can say with practical certainty that the MS. of which they formed a part was written in the second century B.C. and probably near the middle of the century. These fragments, then, are earlier by some hundred years than any other MS. of any part of the Bible, and are, moreover, of more than sentimental interest since they enable us to reach a definite conclusion about the type of text circulating in Egypt about a hundred years after the first translation had been made in Alexandria.'[2] It agrees largely with Theodotion and *Codex Alexandrinus* over against *Vaticanus*, which Hort and Swete had held 'on the whole represents the version of the Septuagint in its relatively oldest form.'[3]

Printed versions of the Greek Old Testament—whether or not they deserve the name of Septuagint—are, of course, common, from the Complutensian Polyglot onwards. In modern times the principal edition in use in this country has been that issued by Dr. Swete of Cambridge, between 1887 and 1894, the introductory volume of which has supplied much material for this chapter. This text is based on *Vaticanus*, wherever it is available, elsewhere upon *Sinaiticus* and *Alexandrinus*. A much larger Cambridge version is still in process of publication. It is based upon the text of Swete, but contains a greatly enlarged critical apparatus of variant readings. The work begun by Origen and Hesychius still goes on.

[1] Sir Frederic Kenyon, *The Text of the Greek Bible* (London, 1949), p. 40.
[2] C. H. Roberts, *op. cit.*, p. 11.
[3] Swete, *op. cit.*, p. 487.

Chapter Ten

SOME IMPORTANT RECENT DISCOVERIES

TWO EVENTS have made great contributions to the study of the Hebrew Old Testament in recent years. The first was the opening up of the Geniza of the Old Cairo Synagogue at the end of the last century. The second has been the even more spectacular discovery of the 'Dead Sea Scrolls' which began in 1947.

A geniza, it will be remembered, was a room adjoining a synagogue used as a receptacle for disused copies of Scripture awaiting ceremonial burial. Here also were placed books which were condemned as heretical, so that it served 'the twofold purpose of preserving good things from harm and bad things from harming.'[1] In his article in the *Times*[2] on the Cairo discoveries, Solomon Schechter described a geniza as a receptacle not for dead and worn-out books alone, but for 'invalid books' in need of repair and for 'disgraced books.' The root of the word *geniza* means to hide or cover up, but in later Hebrew it meant also to store or collect. The term *Apocrypha* or 'hidden' arose to describe those books which were kept in the geniza and not available for public reading. Here also were disused prayer books and any odd leaves on which the name of God might be written. 'All legal documents, such as leases, contracts, marriage settlements and letters of divorce, and the proceedings as well as the decisions of the Courts of justice, were drawn up in Hebrew, or at least, written in Hebrew letters'[3] and anything which looked remotely sacred tended to be put away.

The Cairo Geniza belonged to a Synagogue, which was originally the Christian Church of St. Michael. After the

[1] *Jewish Encyclopaedia*, V. 612.
[2] August 3rd, 1897, 'A Hoard of Hebrew Manuscripts.
[3] *Ibid.*

Saracen conquest it was sold and converted into a Synagogue in A.D. 882—and from that date the accumulation of old literary material began. The Synagogue was rebuilt just over a thousand years later, in 1890, but the Geniza was left unaltered. 'It was by mere chance that the Cairo Geniza was forgotten and that its contents so escaped the fate of other Genizas. Very much against the will of those who had stored them there, these old materials escaped burial. When, in the course of the last century, the Cairo Geniza was rediscovered, the chiefs of the Synagogue to which it belonged made the surprising discovery that there were some curious people in the world who were attracted by the old material, who were also willing to pay a considerable amount of money for these scraps of dirty parchment and paper, and that even renowned universities were interested in it.'[1]

How this material first began to circulate in the West is not known; but some of it is certainly in the collections made by the Russian Jew, Abraham ben Samuel Firkowitzsch. Firkowitzsch was something of a scholar, something of a fanatic, and something of a scoundrel. In the Nineteenth Century he toured Eastern Mediterranean lands, collecting old Hebrew manuscripts, many of whose dates he falsified to give them a fictitious antiquity. He belonged to the sect of the Qaraites, and did everything he could to enhance their prestige, by honest and dishonest means. In the end his whole collection was brought into disrepute; and it is only in recent years that its value has begun to be re-assessed. There can be no doubt, says Kahle, that some of the manuscripts in the second Firkowitzsch collection in Leningrad came from the Cairo Geniza. Also in Russia is the so-called Antonin collection—named after a Russian Archimandrite in Jerusalem—which contains nearly 1,200 fragments from the same source.

In 1864 a Jewish traveller, Jacob Safir, visited the Geniza and later described how he spent two days ferreting among

[1] P. E. Kahle, *The Cairo Geniza*, Schweich Lectures, 1941. (London, O.U.P., 1947), p. 2.

the ancient books and leaves till the dust and ashes sickened him of the task: 'but who knows what may yet be beneath?'[1] From about 1890 the Cairo Jews began to make a general trade with its materials and great quantities were sold. Some reached the Bodleian Library at Oxford. In 1896 Elkan Nathan Adler, brother of the Chief Rabbi, Dr. Hermann Adler, was able actually to enter the Geniza. He brought away a sackful of fragments, of which a certain amount are now in the Library of the Jewish Theological Seminary in New York.

The museums of England owe much to Nineteenth-Century travellers who brought back in their voluminous luggage every kind of curio, from assegais to tombstones. The majority may have been quite uncritical in their acquisitiveness, but some were very perspicacious. Among these were the two sisters from Cambridge, Mrs. Agnes Smith Lewis and Mrs. Margaret Dunlop Gibson, whom we last saw on Mount Sinai in 1892 photographing documents. In 1896 they returned from one of their journeys with fragments from the Geniza. Some were given to the Library of Westminster College, Cambridge. In May, however, they took two leaves to Solomon Schechter, Reader in Talmudic in the University. Schechter was a Roumanian born Jew, who had received his education in Vienna and Berlin, but had come to England in 1882. In 1890 he was appointed a lecturer at Cambridge, and in the following year Reader. He later became President of the Faculty of the Jewish Theological Seminary in the U.S.A. This later development owed much to the two leaves handed to him by Mrs. Lewis and Mrs. Gibson.

One was of parchment and the other of paper. It was the paper fragment which proved really exciting. Schechter found that it contained a portion of the Hebrew text of Ecclesiasticus. This book had its place in the Septuagint and is in the Apocrypha of the English Bible. Worshippers in the Church of England are increasingly accustomed to

---

[1] *Jewish Encyclopaedia, op. cit.*

hearing its sage advice read as the first lesson in Morning or
Evening Prayer. It was known, of course, that the Greek
version of the book was a translation of the original Hebrew,
which must have been written about 200 B.C. No copy of the
Hebrew text had ever turned up. And here it was, on a
scholar's desk in Cambridge. His excitement may be
imagined. There was no air travel in those days; but
Schechter must have quickly begun to enquire about the
speediest sea trip to Egypt.

The Master of St. John's College, Dr. Charles Taylor—
who was not the only Cambridge man to turn from the
study of Mathematics to Oriental Languages—agreed to
finance a visit by Schechter to Cairo. The scholar went with
excitement to his goal. Alexandria disappointed him: there
was little to suggest the city of Philo and the Septuagint.
'Now that the sources of the Nile are being visited by
bicycles,' he wrote, 'there is little fresh to be said about Cairo
and Alexandria.' At Cairo he was given free access to the
Geniza. It had always, he thought, been an integral part
of the Synagogue, but now it was 'situated at the end of the
gallery, presenting the appearance of a sort of windowless
and doorless room of fair dimensions. The entrance is on
the west side, through a big shapeless hole reached by a
ladder.'

Schechter climbed the ladder and looked inside. He saw
what he described as 'a battlefield of books, a battle in
which the literary productions of many generations had
their share, and their *disjecta membra* are now strewn over its
area. Some of the belligerents have perished outright, and
are literally ground to dust in the terrible struggle for space,
whilst others, as if overtaken by a general crush, are squeezed
into big unshapely lumps, which even with the aid of
chemical appliances can no longer be separated without
serious danger to their constituents.'

Where was he to begin? His first decision was not to
collect anything printed. This meant setting on one side
much that might be valuable; but it is doubtful if any other

9

decision could be made. 'The amount of printed fragments is very large,' he wrote, 'constituting as they do nearly all the contributions to the Geniza of the last 400 years. Most of my time in Cairo was spent in getting rid of these *parvenus*, whilst every piece of paper or parchment that had any claim to a respectable age was packed in bags and conveyed to the forwarding agent to be shipped to England. The task was by no means an easy one, the Geniza being very dark, and emitting clouds of dust when the contents are stirred, as if protesting against the disturbance of its inmates. And the protest is the less to be ignored inasmuch as the dust settles in one's throat and threatens suffocation.'

Obviously he needed local help, which was willingly offered, though it raised problems which all who are familiar with the East can imagine. The workmen would not accept a regular wage but sought *bakhshish*. 'Before long the whole population within the precincts of the Synagogue were constantly coming forward with claims on my liberality. All this naturally led to a great deal of haggling and bargaining for which I was sadly unprepared by my former course of life, and which involved a great loss both of money and time.' Nevertheless the 164 boxes handled by the forwarding agents contained about 100,000 fragments for the Cambridge University Library. (There are probably an equal number distributed among other libraries.) The issue of the *Times* which published the remarkable account from which we have taken extracts,[1] contained also a letter from his fellow Cambridge scholar F. C. Burkitt announcing that among the Geniza fragments were parts of the long-lost translation of Aquila. The discovery is hardly more remarkable than the assumptions of biblical literacy made on behalf of the *Times* readers by the writer. 'Your readers will remember,' he writes, 'that this translation was a very literal rendering of the Hebrew made about the middle of the second century of our era for the use of the Greek-speaking Jews who were dissatisfied with the Septuagint.'

[1] August 3rd, 1897.

The material was accepted by the University in November, 1898. The Cairo community received from the Senate of Cambridge University an address in Latin, English and Hebrew which expressed gratitude 'not only on account of the good will with which you received our Reader in Talmudic, but also on account of the conspicuous liberality with which you permitted him to return laden with fragments.'[1] The University's gratitude to Schechter was expressed by his being made a Doctor of Letters, *honoris causa*.

The original starting-point had been Ecclesiasticus: and the publication of the find had led to the discovery of a further nine leaves of the Hebrew text of this book which was in material from the Geniza already in the Bodleian Library at Oxford. Schechter found a further thirteen leaves in Cairo—two of them being from an anthology of extracts. Other leaves of this anthology were identified by Levi in France and by Gaster in London. There are two leaves in the U.S.A. which come from the same manuscript as the eleven found by Schechter in Cairo. All these different portions of the book came originally from the dusty room up the ladder beyond the gallery of the Old Cairo Synagogue. There have been many editions of Ecclesiasticus based upon these finds: for now two-thirds of the book is available in Hebrew; and there are twenty-six Hebrew verses which have no equivalent in Greek. These editions culminated in a great critical version issued by Rudolf Smend in 1906 and 1907.[2]

For textual scholars a great part of the importance of the Geniza discoveries has been the light which they have thrown on the development of the signs (known as points) by which the vowels are indicated in later Hebrew writing. This work is far from being complete. In his lectures to the British

---

[1] Kahle, *op. cit.*, p. 6.

[2] See W. O. E. Oesterley, *Ecclesiasticus*, in the Cambridge Bible for Schools and Colleges (Cambridge, 1912), pp. lxxxvi–xci. The same writer has produced a translation of Ecclesiasticus, incorporating knowledge from the Hebrew text as *The Wisdom of Ben-Sira* in the Translations of Early Documents (London, S.P.C.K., 1916).

Academy on the Cairo Geniza, to which this account owes much, Dr. Kahle of Bonn records Schechter's enthusiasm at Cambridge as he showed his continental visitor the treasures he had secured. 'I saw him sitting in the large room of the Old University Library, surrounded by boxes filled with (at that time) dirty and crumbled fragments, trying to make a first order out of them, and telling me of the little discoveries he was making every day.'[1] Sometimes these were not little but large. It was in the Geniza material that there was found the fragment of the six columns of the Hexapla of Psalm 22. In describing his own work Kahle gave a pleasant reminder of the international nature of scholarship. 'Sometimes', he writes, 'pieces of the same folio are found in different places, as, for instance, a piece of a folio in Cambridge of which the rest is in New York, which contains parts of Proverbs 26 and 27. By chance I had the pieces of the same leaf from Cambridge and New York at the same time in Bonn and could provide the libraries with photographs of the whole leaf of which they possess fragments.'[2]

The story of these finds in Cairo is little known to the general public. The more spectacular discovery in 1947 of the 'Dead Sea Scrolls' has been trumpeted around the world. The happenings are recent; but they are obscured, like ancient chronicles, by conflicting accounts of the same events, so that an accurate statement of what took place is extraordinarily difficult to achieve. Human warfare has always been as great an enemy of the preservation of documents as the natural processes of animal and vegetable decay. Had not the Saracens captured Caesarea Origen's Hexapla might still exist. It is ironical that the great discovery of pre-Massoretic Hebrew texts should take place at the very moment when the British were relinquishing the Palestine mandate and that documents which had been preserved in safety for two thousand years should at once be subjected to the perils and hazards of warfare.

[1] *Op. cit.*, p. 39.   [2] *Ibid.*, p. 46.

The story is this. In the Spring of 1947 an Arab goatherd, in the wild and stony desert towards the Dead Sea—about fifteen miles south of Jericho—noticed a hole among the rocks and idly threw a stone into it. As it fell he heard the sound of pottery breaking. He called his mate and they followed one another on hands and knees into what proved to be a considerable cave. A second opening above their heads served as window, and, as they became accustomed to the darker light they saw around them not only a good deal of broken earthenware but also a number of tall jars which were quite undamaged. It was disappointing that these contained neither gold nor jewels but only leather rolls, containing writing, wrapped up in black cloth.

These men were bedouin Arabs. They had never heard of archaeology: but they may have heard that Europeans were prepared to give money for old writing. And naturally they were on the make. They took four of the rolls away; two each. One they offered to a dealer in Bethlehem, asking £20 for it; but he said this was too much. They met another dealer, a Syrian, who talked the matter over with business associates in Jerusalem. And so the news got round to the Syrian Metropolitan of the Monastery of Saint Mark in Jerusalem. The merchant was told to get hold of the Arabs so that the Monastery might buy the lot. In July they turned up with further specimens. Unfortunately the monk on duty at the gate, who had never heard of the discoveries, sent the men away. They were 'rough-looking Bedouin who had with them some very dirty rolls, several wrapped in dirty cloth with a black substance on them.'[1] The monk glanced at the writing: it was not in Syriac, so he was not interested.

All this came up in the refectory at lunch: it can be imagined how the Metropolitan felt. Where had the men gone? It was discovered that they had gone straight to the market-place, where a Jewish merchant offered to buy the

[1] G. R. Driver, *The Hebrew Scrolls* (Friends of Dr. Williams's Library Lecture, 1950. Oxford University Press, 1951), p. 7.

scrolls for a considerable sum of money. They must go with him to his office where he would get it. The men at once suspected a trick. They would be arrested as spies and put into prison. They fled post haste towards Bethlehem. One of them was persuaded to return; and in the end the Monastery bought five rolls from him—subsequently classified as four, as two belonged to one document.

Meanwhile Professor Sukenik of the Hebrew University had heard about the scrolls and seen a fragment in the possession of a dealer. He managed to get hold of a dealer in Bethlehem who had bought the scrolls from the other Arab who had not returned to do business in dangerous Jerusalem. This was on November 29th, 1947, the very day upon which the United Nations decided upon the partition of Palestine. It was a risky journey back to Jerusalem with his precious purchases: but he got them back safely in the end. The Professor had heard also of the manuscripts which were in the possession of the Syrian Monastery: and funds were available to buy them. In the midst of warfare some of the scrolls were brought to him on neutral ground, so that he could examine them before the final decision was made. He quickly recognised that one of them contained the Book of Isaiah. He was able to copy a number of passages before they were returned to the Monastery. In the end the Metropolitan decided not to sell, but to await calmer times for a calmer appraisal of the value of what he had secured.

In February, 1948, one of the monks took two of the scrolls to the American School of Oriental Research in Jerusalem. A first artful telephone message stated that, in re-cataloguing the Monastery Library five rolls written in archaic Hebrew had been found; and expert help was needed in identifying them. But when he brought them to the School he soon told the true story of their finding. The official in charge, Dr. J. C. Trever, obtained permission to copy some lines from the longest scroll. He also was startled to recognise that it was Isaiah. Could he photograph the

PLATE VII

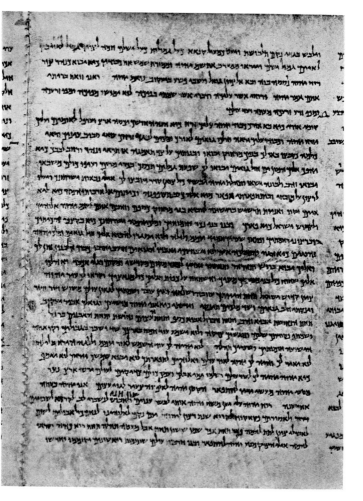

Part of the Scroll of Isaiah from the Dead Sea Cave

documents? Permission was refused for a long time; but he persisted, pointing out that if the contents of the scrolls were made known to the scholars of the world their monetary value would be much increased. At last permission was granted and Dr. Trever spent four days photographing the scrolls column by column. One was not yet in a condition for this as it could not be unrolled. Later the Metropolitan agreed that such valuable and unique possessions should be taken right away from the scene of war. So they were transported to the United States—'none too soon', as Dr. Driver points out, 'for the monastery was badly damaged in the subsequent fighting and Fr. Sowmy, who had most to do with the negotiations about them, was killed.'[1] Publication was handed over to Hebrew scholars in America; and in the Spring of 1950 a first volume containing photographs and transcriptions of the Book of Isaiah and a Commentary on Habakkuk was issued.

Professor Sukenik had already copied out some passages from the roll of Isaiah; and when the Constituent Assembly of the State of Israel met in 1948 each member received a handsome pamphlet containing Chapter Forty taken from the newly-discovered text.[2] 'Comfort ye, comfort ye my people, saith your God. Speak ye comfortably to Jerusalem, and cry unto her, that her warfare is accomplished, that her iniquity is pardoned: for she hath received of the Lord's hand double for all her sins.' To the religiously-minded among the Members the words must have appeared singularly apposite, even though, as in the days of the return from Babylon, they seemed as markedly in conflict with circumstances.

What are the contents of these rolls from the cave? The documents belonging to the Monastery of St. Mark, now in America, are a complete scroll of Isaiah, a commentary on Habakkuk, and what is known as the 'sectarian document', an account of the religious group whose library was

---

[1] *Ibid.*, p. 11.
[2] See Bleddyn J. Roberts, in *Religion in Education*, Autumn, 1949, p. 7.

stored away—for safety in times of crisis—in the cave and the rules by which it lived. This last bears striking similarities with what has been called *Fragments of a Zadokite Work* found by Schechter in the Cairo Geniza, which has been very variously dated by scholars.[1] The scrolls owned by the Hebrew University are six. There is an apocalyptic book entitled *War of the Sons of Light and the Sons of Darkness*, there is a further portion of Isaiah, and there are four rolls containing psalms or hymns entitled *The Praises of the Lord*. Archaeologists were able to visit the cave itself in the Spring of 1949, where they found 'remains of about 40 jars in all, and the manuscripts include portions (most of them very small) of the books of Genesis, Exodus, Leviticus, Deuteronomy, Judges and some books of the Apocrypha.'[2]

The attempt to date these documents has some unusual features. Much was made at first of the jars in which they were stored. Scholars declared that they could hardly have been made later than the Third Century B.C. That, of itself, of course proved nothing. Modern books are often put in much older bookcases. Further investigation revealed that jars of this type were also made a good deal later. What of the religious sect, with its special discipline, whose well-used library was hidden away? This is at the present moment a subject of most learned debate, in which the Zadokite fragments from the Geniza are playing their part. What of the crisis or catastrophe which led to the hiding of the books? It is referred to in the 'sectarian document' and Professor Dupont Sommer of Paris is convinced that it was the capture of Jerusalem by Pompey in 63 B.C.[3] If so, the roll of Isaiah which was hidden away would be just such a one as Jesus opened to read in the Synagogue in Nazareth! But Professor Driver of Oxford points out that 'Palestine has had a long and troubled history, and the fugitives who hid these Scrolls in the cave

---

[1] See H. H. Rowley, *The Covenanters of Damascus and the Dead Sea Scrolls* (Manchester: John Rylands Library, 1952), *passim*.
[2] *Religion in Education, op. cit.*
[3] *The Dead Sea Scrolls* (Blackwell, Oxford, 1952), p. 27.

near Jericho might be fleeing not from the persecution which Antiochus Epiphanes set in motion (165 B.C.) nor from the invasions of the Romans (63 B.C., A.D. 70 and 135) nor even from those of the Persians (A.D. 614) or of the Arabs (A.D. 637) but perhaps merely from some local tumult caused by racial or religious hatred of which history has preserved no record.'[1]

There is evidence also from the cloth in which the scrolls were wrapped. A portion of this has been submitted to the 'radio-carbon test'. This could not be applied to the documents themselves because the material has first to be burned before it will yield its dubious evidence. 'The test was carried out on a sample of the cloth wrappings found in the cave, and it established a mean date of A.D. 33 for the material from which the cloth was made, with a margin of error of two hundred years either way.'[2]

More normal evidence is taken from the rolls themselves, which are made of leather, and not of parchment, and appear to have been well used and repaired. There is a possibility of evidence from the ink. The nature of the writing is important. This is in the square script of modern Hebrew, but in a style which is held to be early. The writing contains an unusually large number of *matres lectionis*, or consonants employed to suggest the vowel sounds for which Hebrew had no letters—the predecessors of the later 'pointing'—and this is thought by some to suggest a time when Hebrew was no longer a spoken language. The books of hymns owned by the Hebrew University are rather biblical pastiche than biblical material: they are full of biblical phrases and variations upon well-known themes, like Seventeenth Century Puritan writing. This, and Aramaic influences which have been discerned, suggest a late date rather than an early one. The text of *War of the Sons of Light and the Sons of Darkness* is similarly full of Old Testament tags. The commentary upon Habakkuk

---

[1] *Op. cit.*, p. 50.
[2] H. H. Rowley in *The Expository Times*, Sept. 1952, p. 379.

suggests a post-Christian date: for it was only with the beginning of the Christian era that the Hebrew canon of Scripture became fixed; and the commentary treats it as an old book, which it expands allegorically. Nevertheless it does give us the oldest text of Habakkuk that we possess. It also omits the third chapter, which scholars have long held to be a later addition.

The roll of Isaiah at Jerusalem has proved extremely difficult to unroll, and only portions have yet been published. The scroll belonging to the Monastery and published in America is in much better preservation. It 'measures exactly 7·34 metres when it is opened out; its average height is about 26 cm. It is made up of 17 pieces of leather sewn end to end; many of these pieces have been re-sewn together in the past, which proves that the roll has been used a great deal. Throughout the roll there are 44 columns of writing each containing 29–32 lines. The writing is clear and on the whole very legible; in several places there are corrections or additions which are in a different hand from the original manuscript. The text of this scroll gives us in full the 66 chapters of the canonical book.'[1]

Professor Dupont Sommer believes that the scrolls are from the First Century B.C. Professor Driver argued for a date in the Seventh or Eighth Century A.D.[2] Later he amended this to a time between A.D. 200 and 500. Professor Kahle believes that they may be dated between the Second and Fourth Centuries A.D. Professor Rowley brings forward considerations which make it 'improbable that the deposit in the cave was later than A.D. 250, and leave open the possibility that it was a good deal earlier.' He believes that the documents could not have been copied out later than A.D. 200.[3]

So we are back many centuries before the Massoretes made their standard editions of the text. What do we find? 'Contrary to what might be expected', writes Professor

---

[1] *The Dead Sea Scrolls*, p. 19.
[2] *The Hebrew Scrolls*, p. 47 & n.
[3] *Expository Times, op. cit.*, p. 380.

Bleddyn Roberts, of the Isaiah scroll, 'its similarity to the
present Massoretic text is astounding. Verse by verse,
frequently word for word the texts are similar. They are
not identical—actually there are reasons for stating that
the new text is a different recension from the Massoretic,
but the essential similarity testifies to the solidarity of the
tradition of the Massoretes.'[1] Professor Sommer writes,
'Failing differences of major importance, what an abundant
harvest of minor variants! . . . Take, for example, Isaiah
52.13–53.12—the well-known poem on the sufferings of the
Servant of the Lord. In these 15 verses I counted as many as
34 actual variants in scroll A. In the light of these variants
it is clear that in future it will be necessary to re-examine the
exegesis of this very difficult passage.'[2]

The story is not yet finished. After the fighting in Palestine died down in 1949 the cave of the scrolls was re-dis-
covered by an expedition of the Arab Legion specially
despatched to the area. Further expeditions, from France,
the U.S.A. and the Kingdom of Jordan, examined over
forty other caves in the neighbourhood. Much pottery was
found and some further fragments of manuscript. 'But the
most exciting find was two rolled-up sheets of bronze on
which a long text in either Hebrew or Aramaic had been
hammered. So far, it has not been possible to read this, and
experiments are going on to try to establish whether it will
be possible to unroll these sheets, the metal of which has
completely oxidised, or whether they will have to be cut
into strips in order to reveal their secret.'[3]

The bedouin Arabs also, who had made the first discoveries, organised their own independent searches, and, in
due course, had the good fortune to find another cave, about
half a mile from the first one, containing an even larger
quantity of Biblical scrolls. They now knew the value of
what they had found. The danger was that a number would
be sold clandestinely and passed into some kind of black

[1] *Religion in Education, op. cit.,* p. 9.
[2] *Op. cit.,* pp. 22, 23. Scroll A is the one owned by the Syrian Monastery.
[3] G. Lankester Harding, in *Picture Post,* 8th August, 1953.

market for export from the country. The Hashemite Kingdom of Jordan, however, managed to raise sufficient funds
to keep them at home: and in the end they will be exhibited
in the Archaeological Museum in Ammam. The Director
of Antiquities for the Kingdom is an Englishman, Dr. G.
Lankester Harding; and at the time of writing, he has a
small exhibition of manuscripts in the British Museum.
Meanwhile the work of photographing and preparation
goes on. 'Biblical scholars the world over', he writes, 'will
be kept busy for the next generation at least pondering and
discussing the translation and significance of these unique
documents, the discovery of which is perhaps the most
sensational and outstanding archaeological event of our
time.'[1]

The remains of at least seventy different scrolls have been
found in this second cave. Thirty-eight are Old Testament
books. Here are Genesis, Exodus, Deuteronomy, Leviticus,
Numbers, Joshua, Ruth, Samuel, Kings, Psalms, Ecclesiastes, Song of Solomon, Isaiah, Jeremiah, Lamentations,
Ezekiel, Daniel, the Minor Prophets; and Tobit, in whole
or in part. Tobit is found for the first time in Hebrew and
Aramaic: before it was only found in a Greek translation
and in versions derived from it. So this appears to follow
Ecclesiasticus as a book of the Apocrypha for which modern
discoveries have provided a text in the original language.

New evidence is available of date, from coins found on the
site, and from the effects of earthquake damage which are
evident. It now appears most likely that the sect which
owned these manuscripts belonged to the movement of the
Essenes, an unorthodox Jewish movement which had some
influence on the development of Christianity. It has been
suggested that John the Baptist lived and studied with the
Essenes; perhaps these very wilderness dwellers whose
library has been brought to light. Others believe that they
were Ebionites, a Jewish-Christian sect with an anti-Pauline
bias. The case for this was argued by Dr. J. L. Teicher, of

[1] *Ibid.*

PLATE VIII

(*Palestine Archaeological Museum*)

Jars in which 'Dead Sea Scrolls' were Found

Cambridge, in the *Manchester Guardian* of September 15th, 1953. A leader writer in the same issue rightly remarks that 'The issues are of great importance, therefore, for New Testament studies, whether these texts are regarded as shedding light on the background of Christianity or on its early history. At first the finds greatly excited Old Testament scholars, but it is now being seen that they are of much more importance to those who are concerned with the New.'

We have travelled a long way, from the Authorised Version to these finds of ancient documents reported in daily newspapers and popular magazines. We have also been taken into areas of lively modern debate. Nor need we doubt that other documents will come to light from deserts and mountains and caves and dens of the earth. Our journey *Back to the Bible* has taken us far nearer the original writing than would have appeared possible a generation ago. It still remains, however, to evaluate the significance of what we have found on our way.

Chapter Eleven

USING WHAT HAS BEEN FOUND

WHEN THE Caliph Othmann fixed a text of the Koran and destroyed all the old copies which differed from his standard, he provided for the uniformity of subsequent manuscripts at the cost of their historical foundation.'[1] If our study has taught us anything it is that nothing like this has happened with the New Testament. There is no standard text. There are multitudes of manuscripts in a surprising number of languages, differing in detail sentence by sentence. Yet if the detailed differences are many the substantial agreement is overwhelming. 'It cannot be repeated too often', wrote Westcott in explaining the changes brought about by the Revised Version, 'that the text of the New Testament surpasses all other Greek texts in the antiquity, variety and fulness of the evidence by which it is attested. About seven-eighths of the words are raised above all doubt by a unique combination of authorities; and of the questions which affect the remaining one-eighth a great part are simply questions of order and form, and such that serious doubt does not appear to touch more than one-sixtieth part of the whole text.'[2]

This judgment has not been disturbed by discoveries made since Westcott's time. In an Introduction to the Revised Standard Version of the New Testament, issued in the U.S.A. in 1946, Professor F. C. Grant wrote: 'It will be obvious to the careful reader that still in 1946, as in 1881 and 1901,[3] no doctrine of the Christian faith has been affected by the revision, for the simple reason that, out of

[1] B. F. Westcott, *Some Lessons of the Revised Version of the New Testament* (4th edition, London, 1903), p. 8.
[2] *Ibid.*, p. 209.
[3] 1881 is the date of the Revised Version, 1901 that of the first American Standard Version derived from it.

the thousands of variant readings in the manuscripts, none
has turned up thus far that requires a revision of the Christian doctrine. At the same time, their variety takes us back
to the great days of freedom and private initiative, when
Christians copied out their own Gospels and Epistles, and
occasionally made mistakes in doing so, and occasionally
added some words to their copies for the sake of complete-
ness—days when martyrdom was still common, and
a victorious Church was superbly "alive and on the
march".'[1]

With the Hebrew Old Testament, as we have seen,
something much more like the fixing of the text of the
Koran by the Muslim Caliph took place through the
intensive labours of the Massoretes. But even their productions were not so uniform as was once thought, and they
are now being checked by newly-discovered manuscripts.
They have long been checked also by the versions, in Greek,
Latin, Syriac, etc., which go back to earlier Hebrew texts
and which provide much variety and some additions. A
further source of testing, for both Testaments and, indeed,
for the Apocrypha, is provided by the quotations of
Scripture in early Christian writers. These men had not
necessarily modern standards of exactness. They did not
unwind a papyrus roll nor find their place in an unwieldy
codex before they quoted. Very largely they quoted from
memory, little thinking that it would be held against them
more than a thousand years later. They provide a most
valuable testimony to the Biblical text: from their pages
the painstaking scholar might reconstruct nearly the whole
of the New Testament and much of the rest of the
Scriptures.[2]

In the most recent full-scale commentary on St. Mark's
Gospel in Greek, by Dr. Vincent Taylor, several pages of
the Introduction are given up to a list of the authorities for

[1] *An Introduction to the Revised Standard Version of the New Testament* (International Council of Religious Education, U.S.A., 1946), p. 42.
[2] 'The quotations from the LXX in the Greek Fathers are an almost unworked
field.' Swete, in 1900, could quote this saying of Hatch in 1889 and say that
it was still true. He did a good deal himself to supply the lack.

the text.[1] The list is not exhaustive: for a fuller treatment the reader is referred elsewhere.[2] But it is large enough for our purposes. It gives a fair idea for the authority for any one book of the New Testament. It is to be remembered also that Mark was little used in the early Church, being over-shadowed by Matthew; and it was presumably less often copied.

The first heading is 'Greek Manuscripts' and the first sub-heading *Uncial MSS*. The word *uncial*, it will be re-called, refers to the earlier form of Greek writing, in what we should call capital letters, while *cursive* refers to the running hand, more like our own handwriting, which developed later and was used more for personally owned copies of Scripture than for those owned by Churches and used in public worship. Under this sub-heading there are listed sixteen manuscripts, dating from the Fourth to the Ninth or possibly Tenth Century. They are headed by *Sinaiticus* (א), *Alexandrinus* (A) and *Vaticanus* (B) all of which contain the whole Gospel. This is also be be found in five of the other manuscripts. The rest contain only parts.

The next sub-heading is *Papyrus*: and here we learn that the Chester Beatty manuscript of the Third Century (P[45]) contains parts of eight chapters of this Gospel. Next come *Minuscules*, cursive manuscripts containing this Gospel dating from the Ninth to the Fifteenth Century. These manuscripts are listed not by letter but by number—and it is well to remember Streeter's *caveat* that 'many cursives are quite as important as any uncials after the first five אBLDΘ; the practice of citing uncials by a capital letter, cursives by a number, makes the difference between them appear far greater than it really is.'[3] Twelve of these numeri-cal references are given. The first two, however, refer to families of inter-related documents, so that a great many

---

[1] *The Gospel According to St. Mark. The Greek Text with Introduction, Notes, and Indexes*, by Vincent Taylor, Ph.D., D.D., Principal of Wesley College, Leeds (London, 1952), pp. 33–37.

[2] See Legg, *Novum Testamentum Graece*.

[3] *The Four Gospels* (London, 1924), p. 28.

more than twelve actual manuscripts are in question. Like the uncials, these are scattered across the world, from the U.S.S.R. to the U.S.A.

From Greek we turn to the Latin versions, and the first sub-heading is *The Old Latin*. These are indicated by small letters. Twenty different manuscripts are listed, dating from the Fourth Century to the Twelfth. Nine of these contain the whole Gospel. Next comes *The Vulgate*; and here this commentary refers only to the edition of the Vulgate text prepared by J. Wordsworth and H. J. White. The manuscripts of the Vulgate are, of course, very numerous.

Other versions follow. First comes the *Syriac*. Five authorities are given, dating from the Fourth to the Seventh Century. Two of these contain the whole Gospel: one, the Fifth Century *Peshitta*, has it in many manuscripts. There follow the *Egyptian*, *Georgian*, *Armenian* and *Aethiopic*, smaller groups of documents, dating from the Third Century to the Ninth. All this evidence is buttressed by the *Ecclesiastical Writers*, from the Second to the Fifth Century, who quote St. Mark; and a list of twenty-six of these authorities is given.

Let us see how this information is used. There are two significant passages in Mark where it can suitably be tested. The first is the opening verse. The Revised Version renders this, 'The beginning of the gospel of Jesus Christ, the Son of God', but adds in the margin, 'Some ancient authorities omit *the Son of God*.' What has Dr. Taylor to say about this? Here is a part of his note, which we must do our best to understand:

> υἱοῦ θεοῦ is omitted by אℵ* Θ 28 sy^hier geo¹ arm Iren Or, and by the WH text. There are strong reasons, however, for accepting the phrase as original, in view of its attestation (אℵ^a B D L W it vg sy ^pe hl sa bo geo² arm (3 best MSS.) Iren Or^int Aug), its possible omission by homoioteleuton, and the use of the title in Mark's Christology.*

* *Ibid.*, p. 152.

The interpretation of this concentrated scholarship is roughly as follows. The words which the Revised Version renders 'the Son of God' are omitted by *Sinaiticus*, from the important Koridethi manuscript (now at Tiflis) dating from some time between the Seventh and Ninth Centuries, by a cursive manuscript at Paris which dates from the Eleventh or Twelfth Century, by the Sixth Century Syriac lectionaries from Jerusalem (edited by Mrs. Lewis and Mrs. Gibson), by one of the Georgian versions, and by one of the Fifth Century Armenian versions. In quoting St. Mark, Irenaeus and Origen omitted the words, and when Westcott and Hort prepared their text in the Nineteenth Century they felt constrained to leave them out. Turning from Dr. Taylor to Hort's volume of *Introduction* to their version one finds that the two editors considered the balance of probability to be very slight. 'Omission, possibly Alexandrian, is certainly of high antiquity. On the whole it seems to deserve the preference: but neither reading can be safely rejected.'[1]

We return to our interpretation of Dr. Taylor. 'There are strong reasons, however, for accepting the phrase as original, in view of its attestation'. . . . Although it was not in the original of *Sinaiticus* it was added by the first corrector of this document. (We remember the claim that it had been collated with a very ancient manuscript which had been corrected by a disciple of Origen, who had compared it with the Hexapla itself.) It is to be found in *Vaticanus*, *Bezae*, *Regius* (an Eighth Century manuscript at Paris) and in the Fifth Century *Washington Codex*. Both the Peshitta and the Harcleian versions of the Syriac contain it. So do both Sahidic and Bohairic versions in Egypt and one of the Georgian versions. The three best manuscripts of the Armenian give it. Though not quoted by Irenaeus and Origen, when their works were translated into Latin, probably in the Fourth Century, the words were given. Augustine also

[1] *The New Testament in the Original Greek.* The text revised by Brooke Foss Westcott, D.D., and Fenton John Anthony Hort, D.D. *Introduction* (Cambridge & London, 1882). Appendix, p. 23.

in the Fourth Century gave them. It is further suggested that the words might have originally been omitted by a natural copyist's slip, as the genitive of Christ, in the Greek, and the genitive of God both end with the same letters. A further suggestion is that the use of the phrase fits in with what we know of Mark's theological attitude to Christ.

The second test in St. Mark's Gospel concerns its ending. If we turn to Mark 16.8 in the Revised Version we find that a gap is introduced before the next verse and a note is added in the margin to verse 9. 'The two oldest Greek manuscripts and some other authorities, omit from ver. 9 to the end. Some other authorities have a different ending to the Gospel.' The American Revised Standard Version goes further and exiles the whole of verses 9–20 to the margin, adding to this 'Longer Ending' the 'Shorter Ending'. This reads: 'But they reported briefly to Peter and those with him all that they had been told. And after this, Jesus Himself sent out by means of them, from east to west, the sacred and imperishable proclamation of eternal salvation.' Mark, certainly, would have had to have suffered a sea-change to have produced such phrasing! Those who have studied the Greek of verses 9 to 20 as it is found in the Textus Receptus find there also a vocabulary very different from what was normal to Mark.

Nevertheless, it would be strange that a book which began with the words 'the beginning of the Good News' should end 'for they were afraid'. Nor can Mark have meant to end his Gospel without some account of an appearance of Jesus to the Disciples in Galilee, which is prophesied both in 14.28 and in 16.7. Many suggestions have been made to account for this 'lost ending' of Mark. It seems likeliest that it was just broken off. The ends of much-used books are always in danger, as anyone who has had to look up the Y.M.C.A. in the telephone directory of a public call-box must know. 'The two ends of a roll would always be exposed to damage; the beginning ran the greater risk, but, in a book rolled from both ends, the conclusion was not safe.'[1] When Christians were a persecuted group of people, in danger of their lives, their property always in danger of disturbance or seizure by state officials, it would not be surprising if a valued possession should get damaged. If this happened, however, it must have happened early. There is no indication in the use made in Matthew and Luke of Mark that the authors of these Gospels had any fuller Gospel before them than the one we know, ending at 16.8. Eusebius also, whom Streeter describes as 'the most widely read scholar of Christian antiquity,'[2] recorded, *c.* 325, that in the oldest and best manuscripts of St. Mark known to him the Gospel ended with the words 'for they were afraid.' Jerome gives a similar report.

What of the manuscript evidence? 'The two oldest Greek manuscripts' referred to in the Revised Version margin, which excluded verses 9 to 20, are *Sinaiticus* and *Vaticanus*. (Both are listed by Vincent Taylor as containing 'the whole Gospel'; but he does not regard this 'longer ending' as an integral part of it.) They are omitted by the Old Latin *Codex Bobiensis* (k) a Fourth or Fifth Century manuscript preserved at Turin, which gives instead the Shorter Ending. The Fourth Century Syriac from Mount Sinai omits them also. They are absent from the three best Armenian manuscripts: a fourth, rather excitingly, contains this ending, separated off, with the heading 'Of the Presbyter Ariston.' In the oldest Georgian manuscript, dated A.D. 897, the Longer Ending is added as 'a sort of Appendix to the Four Gospels after the end of John, having been apparently copied from another text.'[3]

The Shorter Ending is found in *Codex Regius* (Eighth Century, Paris), *Codex Laurensis* (Eighth or Ninth Century, Mount Athos) and in the Thirteenth Century minuscule, 579, in Paris. It is in the Sahidic and Aethiopic versions and in the Old Latin k from Africa. It is also in two uncial

---

[1] Streeter, *op. cit.*, p. 338.
[2] *Ibid.*, p. 335.
[3] *Ibid.*

fragments and in the margin of one Greek cursive. It is in the Harcleian Syriac and in the oldest manuscripts of the Bohairic. In the Greek manuscripts and in most of the translations—but not in k—the Longer Ending usually follows the Shorter, being introduced by the words 'this is also current.' The Washington manuscript contains an ending of its own; though part of it is quoted by Jerome as found in some manuscripts. This reads, after verse 14 of the Longer Ending, in which Jesus upbraided the disciples because of their unbelief:

And they replied saying, this age of lawlessness and unbelief is under Satan, who does not allow what is under the unclean spirits to comprehend the true power of God; therefore reveal thy righteousness. Already they were speaking to Christ; and Christ told them in addition that the limit of the years of the authority of Satan has been fulfilled, but other terrible things are at hand, even for the sinners on whose behalf I was delivered up to death, that they might turn to the truth and sin no more, in order that they may inherit the heavenly spiritual incorruptible glory of righteousness.[1]

This is hardly a passage which authenticates itself.

Hort declared that in the whole of Greek literature before the period of the Council of Nicaea (A.D. 325) there were at most two traces of verses 9–20. Yet one of these is in Irenaeus. Around A.D. 185 he quoted from 16.19 as 'from the end of Mark.'

This means that the Longer Ending was written before the end of the Second Century. Tatian also, in producing his Diatessaron, or harmony of the Gospels, c. A.D. 170, used this ending. Yet it is rejected by the earliest uncials. 'Since B ℵ were written in the fourth century', writes Streeter, both the Longer and Shorter Conclusions were already of great antiquity and can hardly have been unknown to the scribes who wrote these MSS. and, for that

[1] *Ibid.*, p. 337.

matter, to a fairly long succession of MSS. from which they were copied.' He goes on to remark that 'an asceticism which could decline to accept either of these endings argues a fidelity to a text believed to be more ancient, which materially increases our general confidence in the textual tradition which these MSS. represent.'[1] In conclusion we may, with Dr. Taylor, agree that the Revised Standard Version is fully justified in relegating the passage to the margin.[2]

As work on biblical documents, and on other ancient documents, has gone forward, there have been developed reliable methods of textual criticism, which some writers have even named a science. The problem to be faced has, we hope, become clear in the pages of this book. It was very succinctly stated by Hort in his *Introduction*. 'No autograph of any book of the New Testament is known or believed to be still in existence. . . . The books of the New Testament have had to share the fate of other ancient writings in being copied again and again during more than fourteen centuries down to the invention of printing and its application to Greek literature.'[3]

Copyists make mistakes. Those who make further copies usually repeat the mistakes that have already been made and make fresh ones of their own. As the process of study has gone on certain almost standardized mistakes have come to be recognised by critics, as anticipated mistakes are repeated by generation after generation of pupils in their written work and ruefully—or gleefully—detected by school-masters. This is the kind of thing the textual critic is on the look-out for:[4]

(i) Wrong divisions of words. No gaps were made between words in ancient writing, and the wrong gaps might be introduced by later copyists. 'I saw abundance on the

---

[1] *Ibid.*
[2] *Op. cit.*, p. 610.
[3] *Op. cit.*, p. 4.
[4] The list which follows is largely dependent on A. Souter, *The Text & Canon of the New Testament* (London, 1912), pp. 113, 114.

table' might be rendered 'I saw a bun dance on the table'. In a few places in the New Testament this seems to have happened.

(ii) Omission of syllables or words or lines. This is familiar to any reader of proofs. It happens most often where similar words are concerned. 'If the syllables be identical and one is omitted, this error is known as haplography. If the omission be due to the syllable having the same beginning as that next to it, the error is said to be due to *homoioarcton*; if to the possession of the same ending, it is called *homoioteleuton*.'[1] It will be recalled that the possibility of such an error in transcription was discussed in our consideration of Mark 1.1.

(iii) Repetition of syllables or words or lines. This is called *dittography*.

(iv) Transposition of syllables.

(v) Unconscious mental activity on the part of the copyist may lead him to write down words with which he is familiar in place of the actual text before him. The present writer found this happening in typing out this actual chapter. Instead of typing 'private initiative' in the quotation from Professor F. C. Grant on page 141 he discovered that he had used the more familiar term 'private enterprise'! The similarity of the Gospels has been responsible for much hardly conscious approximation of one to another. Writing out a passage in Mark a copyist might naturally adjust it to the form of words in Matthew with which he was more familiar. Sometimes, too, he might just want to improve the grammar. There was good reason for the rabbinic insistence that 'no word or letter, not even a *yod*, must be written from memory, the scribe not having looked at the codex before him' but the same meticulous care was not always exercised by Christians.

(vi) Often illustrative material was written in the margin of a manuscript. A later copyist might take it as an addition and incorporate it in the text. There are a number of places

[1] *Ibid.*, p. 114.

in the New Testament where this is likely to have taken place.

Members of the Church of England, for example, know that when they join in the Lord's Prayer in their Parish Church they may be expected to continue to the doxology 'for thine is the kingdom, the power and the glory, for ever and ever. Amen' or to say their *Amen* more abruptly after 'deliver us from evil'—and many have a not unnatural tendency, like the copyists we have been considering, to supply the doxology where it is lacking. The original prayer is given by Matthew and Luke. In Luke 11.4 the Authorised Version ends 'but deliver us from evil'. When we turn to Matthew 6.13 we find the additional words. But when we go from the Authorised Version to the Revised Version we find that they are put in the margin, introduced by the statement, 'Many authorities, some ancient, but with variations, add, *For thine*, etc.'

The doxology is a very suitable conclusion to the prayer. No doubt it was used in public worship, written into the margin of the biblical text, and inserted into the text itself by a later scribe. Hort writes that 'there can be little doubt that the Doxology originated in liturgical use in Syria, and was thence adopted into the Greek and Syriac Syrian texts of the New Testament.' It may reflect contemporary Jewish usage, as the people's response to prayers in the temple is said to have been 'Blessed be the name of the glory of his kingdom for ever and ever.'[1] Later copyists put it into Luke as well, as we find by looking at the Revised Version marginal note. There we learn also that the best manuscripts of St. Luke omit 'Thy will be done in earth as it is in heaven' and 'deliver us from evil'. Later ones have been assimilated to the Matthean text.

In St. John's Gospel there is to be found the familiar and moving story of the woman taken in adultery. The Revised Version puts this whole passage—from 7.53 to the end of 8.11—into square brackets. There is a note in the margin

[1] *Introduction*, Appendix, p. 9.

saying that 'Most of the ancient authorities omit' this passage. The Revised Standard Version relegates the passage itself to the margin, with the note, 'Most of the ancient authorities either omit 7.53–8.11 or insert it with variations of the text, here or at the end of this gospel or after Luke 21.38.' It is actually omitted by *Sinaiticus, Vaticanus, Alexandrinus, Ephraemi, Regius,* and the *Washington Codex,* as well as by some Old Latin manuscripts, Old Syriac and Sahidic. The manuscript evidence against the Authorised Version is here overwhelming. Add to this the fact that no Greek commentator on the passage before the Twelfth Century makes any reference to the passage and the further fact that its vocabulary and style is distinct from that of the rest of the Gospel, and the conviction that it is an intruder is further enforced. Most scholars think that it was first written into the margin as a comment on 8.15: 'Ye judge after the flesh; I judge no man.'

To say that the story does not really belong to St. John's Gospel is not to say that it is not itself authentic. There are references to the story early. The *Apostolic Constitutions,* in a passage based upon a Third Century Syriac work, 'in the course of warning bishops against too great severity in dealing with sinners, quotes the words of Jesus to the "woman who had sinned"—*neither do I condemn thee*—in order to secure leniency of treatment.'[1] There is no suggestion here that it is the Fourth Gospel which is being quoted. The passage is also marked by a great number of variant readings 'which would be intelligible if it had had a wandering circulation and only found a disciplined home in the canonical gospels at a fairly late date.'[2] It appears, therefore, to be a piece of genuine early tradition about Jesus, for whose preservation we may be very thankful. This is a passage which *does* authenticate itself.

To the types of error we have listed there needs to be added the general principle that a harder reading is usually

[1] Sir Edwyn Hoskyns, *The Fourth Gospel,* edited by F. N. Davey (2nd edition, London, 1947), p. 566.
[2] *Ibid.,* p. 565.

to be preferred to an easier one. At any rate the more difficult reading should be examined a good many times before it is rejected. Difficulties are more often smoothed out by later copyists than deliberately introduced. This is a principle familiar enough to the student of the Synoptic Gospels. The roughnesses of Mark are often smoothed out by Matthew: all the more reason to prefer Mark. Copyists often followed in Matthew's steps.

How may the value of different texts be assessed? It can hardly be enough to find the reading of the majority of manuscripts, to count heads, as it were. A solitary exception might preserve an original reading where all the others were corrupt. Nor is it necessarily enough to find the earliest manuscript. A newer one might be a faithful copy of a much more ancient document. It has been found, very naturally, that variant readings tend to perpetuate themselves in manuscript after manuscript. The important thing therefore is to establish a manuscript's genealogy; to discover from what grandparent or great grandparent it derived its particular characteristics. Thus there has been evolved a classification of families of manuscripts. Scholars believe that by the end of the Second Century there existed five main types of text, and that all existing manuscripts go back to ancestors which are to be found in one of these groups. These have been classified as follows:

(1) Western, represented by *Codex Bezae* and the Old Latin version.

(2) Caesarean, represented by the Koridethi Gospels, etc.

(3) Alexandrian, represented by *Codex Sinaiticus, Codex Vaticanus*, and the Coptic version.

(4) Syriac, represented by the Old Syriac version.

(5) Other, i.e., a classification for readings that do not fall into any of the preceding groups.[1]

The existence of the vague fifth classification is an indication that the work of textual criticism is far from being

---

[1] The list is taken from F. C. Grant, *op. cit.*, p. 39, but is based on the work of Sir Frederic Kenyon.

complete. This newer analysis takes the place of the earlier theories of Westcott and Hort. They thought that they had arrived at a near approach to a 'neutral' text, which lay behind all the others. This is no longer believed: their text is much closer to what is now classed as Alexandrian. Nevertheless their twenty-eight years of combined work on the text of the New Testament marks an epoch in biblical studies and provides a starting point for most textual critics of to-day.

Principles which are nowadays followed have been stated by Professor F. C. Grant in the Introduction to the Revised Standard Version of the New Testament. 'With the best will in the world', he writes, 'the New Testament translator or reviser of today is forced to adopt the eclectic principle: each variant reading must be studied on its merits, and cannot be adopted or rejected by some rule of thumb, or by adherence to such a theory as that of the "Neutral Text".'[1] He gives the following rules to be followed in this procedure:

1. No one type of text is infallible, or to be preferred by virtue of its generally superior authority.

2. Each reading must be examined on its merits, and preference must be given to those readings which are demonstrably in the style of the author under consideration.

3. Readings which explain other variants, but are not contrariwise to be explained by the others, merit our preference; but this is a very subtle process, involving intangible elements, and liable to subjective judgment on the part of the critic.'[2]

The textual criticism of the Old Testament is, in some ways, at a more elementary stage, and, in others, more difficult for the uninstructed to understand. For a long time it was thought that there were very few variants in the actual Hebrew text which had been handed down. This did not prevent critics from making innumerable 'conjectural

---

[1] *Ibid.*, p. 41.   [2] *Ibid.*

emendations' of the text, to explain passages which were difficult or incomprehensible. Very often it was found that the alteration of one letter made all the difference: the practice became something very like a passion—which has been duly chastened by the discovery of new Hebrew texts. Criticism has, of course, made much use of the versions, particularly of the Septuagint, so that the late Professor W. Emery Barnes once complained that the textual criticism of the Bible 'may be broadly described as a starveling science which ekes out its existence on false pretences . . . It lives chiefly by one hypothesis: that a vast number of *renderings* of the Septuagint can be turned back at sight into ancient *readings* of the Hebrew text. Renderings (readings) of other versions are cited at the heel of the Septuagint, but chiefly by way of garnishing.' Professor Bleddyn Roberts, who quotes this plaint, adds that 'during the three decades that have since elapsed, scholars who have specialized in the study of the versions have to some extent adjusted the balance between the Massoretic text and the renderings of the versions, to the mutual advantage of both. A major result of the new evaluation is the extent to which caution is observed in the use of the new versions for emendation purposes.'[1] And the present decade is one in which a new era in the textual criticism of the Old Testament is beginning. There are fresh discoveries yet to be made, and fresh light to be brought to men from all parts of Scripture.

F. J. A. Hort once wrote: 'In respect of the Bible especially, it remains true that whatever helps our understanding helps also in the long run our praying and our working.' His words were quoted by another great scholar, the late Sir Frederic Kenyon.[2] They represent the underlying aim of all that has been written in this book.

[1] *The Old Testament Text and Versions*, p. 272.
[2] *The Text of the Greek Bible*, p. 11.

SHORT CHRONOLOGICAL TABLE

THE manuscripts of the Bible, like those of other ancient books, are all copies of earlier ones. There are no original manuscripts. In recent years much earlier documents have been discovered than those upon which earlier translators of the Bible have relied. This table sets out some of the events and discoveries which have established the present biblical text. The names of actual manuscripts are given in *italics*.

Men and Events	*Documents and Discoveries*
BEFORE CHRIST	
	Third Century B.C. possible date for *Dead Sea Scrolls*.
336–323 The conquests of Alexander the Great made the Greek language a *lingua franca* throughout the Near East.	From the Third Century to the Christian era the Septuagint translation of the Old Testament into Greek was in the making.
285–247 Ptolemy Philadelphus, the ruler of Egypt with whom the legend of the Septuagint is linked.	Second Century B.C. *Fragment of Deuteronomy* in Greek (Rylands Library).
63 Capture of Jerusalem by Pompey. Possible date of hiding of *Dead Sea Scrolls*.	
CHRISTIAN ERA	
	The *Dead Sea Scrolls* are thought by many to be not later than A.D. 200
64 Fire of Rome. Deaths of Peter and Paul.	
70 Destruction of Jerusalem.	
90 Synod of Jamnia establishes the canon of Hebrew Scriptures.	

SECOND CENTURY

Fragment of St. John (Rylands Library).

Chester Beatty Portions of Numbers and Deuteronomy.

Papyrus Fragments of an Unknown Gospel (British Museum).

c. 150 Aquila translated the Old Testament into Greek. Rather later, Theodotion produced a free revision of the LXX.

c. 170 Tatian produced his harmony of the Gospels or 'Diatessaron'.

c. 200 Symmachus makes a further translation of the Old Testament into Greek.

c. 200 suggested date of *Syriac Palimpsest* from Mount Sinai.

c. 120–202 Irenaeus.

'Muratorian Canon' drawn up probably between 160 and 170 is a list containing all the present New Testament books except Hebrews, James, 1 and 2 Peter, and 3 John.

Clement of Alexandria, *c.* 160–*c.* 220.

Tertullian, 160–230.

Origen, 185–254, produces Biblical commentaries and 'Hexapla.'

Eusebius of Caesarea, 264–340.

THIRD CENTURY

Oxyrhynchus Sayings of Jesus.

Chester Beatty Gospels and Acts.

Fragment of the Diatessaron (Yale)

Freer Greek MS. V.

Chester Beatty Genesis.

Chester Beatty Revelation.

Sahidic translations probably made towards the end of the Third Century.

FOURTH CENTURY

303   Persecution of Diocletian.

306   Constantine hailed as Augustus at York, 312 accepted at Rome.

311   Death of Hesychius, 312 death of Lucian, who produced editions of the LXX.

313   Edict of Milan gives freedom of worship to Christians.

324   Constantine sole Emperor.

332   Constantine orders 50 vellum Bibles from Eusebius of Caesarea.

312–380   Bishop Ulfilas, who produces the Gothic Bible.

Important Fourth Century Manuscripts:
    Codex Vaticanus (B)
    Codex Sinaiticus (ℵ),
    Codex Vercellensis (*a*) Old Latin
    Codex Alexandrinus (A) and
    Codex Colberto-Sarravianus (G) are late Fourth or early Fifth Century.

382   Pope Damasus commissions Jerome (*c.* 346–420) to revise the Latin Bible.

383   Jerome's Four Gospels followed by the other books which make the 'Vulgate' translation into Latin.
Late Fourth Century. The Bohairic translations and the Ethiopic Old Testament.

157

Men and Events	Documents and Discoveries

FIFTH CENTURY

Codex Ephraemi (C).

Rabbula, Bishop of Edessa, 401–435, instigates the New Testament Syriac version ('Peshitta').

Manuscript of *Peshitta version of the Pentateuch* in British Museum, dated in the year of the Greeks, 775, i.e. A.D. 442.

Fifth or Sixth Century. *Codex Bezae* (D).

SIXTH CENTURY

c. 545 *Codex Fuldensis* (to Jarrow *c.* 681, then, with Boniface to Germany).

SEVENTH CENTURY

c. 600 Ethiopic New Testament.

638 Capture of Caesarea. Destruction of 'Hexapla.'
Important Names in the Revival of Religion and Scholarship in England:
St. Hilda, at Whitby (658–680) encourages Caedmon.
Theodore of Tarsus, Archbishop of Canterbury (669–690).
Benedict Biscop (*c.* 628–689).
St. Willibrord (658–739).
St. Boniface (674–754).
The Venerable Bede (673–735).

698–721 Production of *Lindisfarne Gospels.*

EIGHTH CENTURY

c. 735–804   Alcuin of York, who establishes scholarship at the Court of Charlemange.

Codex Venetus (V) late Eighth or early Ninth Century.

NINTH CENTURY

(Until recently the earliest Hebrew MSS. belonged to the Ninth Century.)

Koridethi MSS (Θ).

Codex Bodleianus (I).

Cyril (or Constantine) (d. 869) and Methodius (d. 885) originate the Slavonic translations.

848–899   Alfred, King of England, translates portions of the Bible into Anglo-Saxon to incorporate in his Laws.

TENTH CENTURY

The Tenth Century marks the culmination of the work of the Massoretes on the text of the Hebrew Bible.

Aelfric of Bath prepares *Anglo-Saxon Gospels* (at Corpus Christi, Cambridge).

Aelfric of Eynsham (950–1020) translates *selections of Old Testament.*

Aldred adds *Northumbrian gloss* to *Lindisfarne Gospels.*

Palimpsest of *Hexapla Psalms* (Milan).

ELEVENTH CENTURY

1066 Norman Conquest of England.
1069 Destruction of Alcuin's Library at York.
Stephen Harding (1061–1134) makes contact with Jewish scholars (1109) and prepares a revised version of the Vulgate for the Cistercian Order.

TWELFTH CENTURY

1090–1153 St. Bernard.
1179 Third Lateran Council condemns Waldensians.

THIRTEENTH CENTURY

1175–1253 Robert Grosseteste.
1214–1292 Roger Bacon.
In this century the monks of Ramsey Abbey in Huntingdonshire owned the whole Old Testament in Hebrew. Between 1250 and 1350 there appeared Anglo-French and Middle English paraphrases of the Sunday Gospels.

FOURTEENTH CENTURY

1340 d. Nicholas de Lyra, who emphasised the importance of the literal interpretation of the Bible.
1349 d. Richard Rolle of Hampole, whose English prose version of the Psalms was already in use.
John Wycliffe (1328–1384) inspires a literal translation of the Vulgate (1384) followed by a freer version (1385–7).
In the Fourteenth or Fifteenth Century the Old Testament was translated into Castilian.

FIFTEENTH CENTURY

1414   Council of Constance condemns vernacular translations.

1430   Completion of the *Bible of the House of Alba*, a translation into Spanish.

1453   Fall of Constantinople.

1454   Gutenberg uses movable type.

1456   *Latin Bible* printed, the first book to be printed in Europe.

Gianozzo Manetti collects manuscripts for Pope Nicholas V. Pico della Mirandola (1463–1494) interested in Hebrew, and Johann Reuchlin (1455–1522) becomes a pioneer in Hebrew studies.

1474   Caxton begins printing in England.

1477   Hebrew *Psalter* printed (? Bologna).

1482   Hebrew *Law* printed (Bologna).

1482   Hebrew *Prophets* printed (Soncino).

1483   Caxton's edition of *The Golden Legend* includes biblical material.

1487   Hebrew *Writings* printed (Naples).

1496   John Colet lectures on the Greek text of Romans at Oxford.

1498   Erasmus comes to England.

Men and Events	Documents and Discoveries
	SIXTEENTH CENTURY .
1506 Reuchlin's *De Rudimentis Hebraicis*	1502–1517 Preparation of *Complutensian Polyglot* (published 1522).
	1516 Erasmus' *Greek New Testament*.
	SOME IMPORTANT ENGLISH VERSIONS
1530 Burning of Tyndale's New Testaments in St. Paul's.	1525 Tyndale's *New Testament*.
1536 Execution of Tyndale.	1530 Tyndale's *Pentateuch*.
1549 First English Prayer Book.	1535 Coverdale's *Bible*.
1553–1558 Queen Mary sets the clock back.	1539 *The Great Bible*.
	1560 *The Geneva Bible*.
	1582 *The Rheims-Douai Bible* (Roman Catholic).
	1611 *The Authorized Version*.
	1550 Stephanus edition with critical apparatus.
	1551 Stephanus edition with numbered verses.
	1553 Spanish Old Testament printed in Ferrara for the Jews of Salonika.
	SEVENTEENTH CENTURY
1627 *Codex Alexandrinus* brought to England.	1657 Walton's *Polyglot* contains evidence from manuscripts previously unexamined.
	EIGHTEENTH CENTURY

The examination of manuscripts by scholars prepares the way for the great activity of the following century.
1778 Earliest discoveries of papyri in Egypt. One of these is in the Museum at Naples.

NINETEENTH CENTURY

1842 British Museum secures the *Curetonian Syriac Gospels* (published 1858).

1844 Tischendorf pays his first visit to the Monastery of St. Catherine on Mount Sinai.

1850 Tischendorf edits *Codex Amiatinus*.

1852 Tischendorf edits *Codex Claromontanus*.

1853 Westcott and Hort begin work on their edition of the Greek New Testament.

1859 Tischendorf begins negotiations to secure *Codex Sinaiticus*.

1864 Jacob Safir visits the Cairo Geniza.

1877 First large discoveries of papyri.

1881 Revised Version: New Testament.

1881 Westcott and Hort's *Greek New Testament*.

1884 Revised Version: Old Testament.

1895 Revised Version: Apocrypha.

1897 Solomon Schechter visits the Cairo Geniza and brings spoils to Cambridge.

TWENTIETH CENTURY

1930–31 *Chester Beatty Papyri*.

1934 *Fragments of an Unknown Gospel* (British Museum).

1936 Early Fragments of *St. John* and Deuteronomy (Rylands Library).

1946 *Revised Standard Version N.T.* (U.S.A.) (O.T. 1952).

1947 First discovery of *Dead Sea Scrolls*.

BIBLIOGRAPHY

ADAMSON, John William, *The Illiterate Anglo-Saxon* (Cambridge, 1946).

BARROW, R. H., *The Romans* (London, Penguin Books, 1949).

BEDE, The Venerable, *The Ecclesiastical History of the English Nation* (Everyman edition, 1951).

BETTENSON, Henry, *Documents of the Christian Church* (Oxford, World's Classics, 1943).

BRADLEY, Henry, *The Goths* (Heroes of the Nations series, London, 1888).

BROWN, John, *History of the English Bible* (Cambridge, 1911).

BURCKHARDT, Jacob, *The Renaissance in Italy* (London, fourth edition, 1898).

CLAPPERTON, R. H., *Modern Paper-making*, ch. i, 'The History of Paper-making' (Oxford, third edition, 1952).

COULTON, G. G., *Five Centuries of Religion*, vol. iii (Cambridge, 1936).

The Codex Sinaiticus and the Codex Alexandrinus (London, British Museum, 1951).

DEANESLY, Margaret, *The Lollard Bible* (Cambridge, 1920).
The Significance of the Lollard Bible (Univ. of London, The Athlone Press, 1951).

DEMAUS, R., *William Tyndale* (London, 1887).

DRIVER, G. R., *The Hebrew Scrolls* (Oxford, 1951).

Fragments of an Unknown Gospel and Other Early Papyri (London, British Museum, 1935).

FROUDE, J. A., *Life and Letters of Erasmus* (London, Silver Library edition, 1910).

GWATKIN, H. M., *Early Church History* (London, 1909).

HARDING, G. Lankester, article in *Picture Post*, 8th August, 1953.

HARNACK, Adolf, *Bible Reading in the Early Church* (London, 1912).

HARRISON, Frederick, *Life in a Medieval College* (London, 1952).

HOSKYNS, Sir Edwyn, *The Fourth Gospel*, edited F. N. Davey (second edition, London, 1947).

Introduction to the Revised Standard Version of the New Testament (International Council for Religious Education, U.S.A., 1946).

Introduction to the Revised Standard Version of the Old Testament (London, 1952).

JAMES, M. R., *The Christian Renaissance*, Chapter xvii in *Cambridge Modern History*, vol. i (Cambridge, 1903).

The Apocryphal New Testament (Oxford, 1924).

Jewish Encyclopaedia, vol. v, article, *Geniza*.

JUSSERAND, J. J., *A Literary History of the English People* (London, 1895).

KAHLE, P. E., *The Cairo Geniza* (London, 1949).

KENYON, Sir Frederic, *Our Bible and the Ancient Manuscripts* (fourth edition, London, 1939).

The Text of the Greek Bible (London, 1949).

LATOURETTE, K. S., *A History of the Expansion of Christianity*, vol. i (London, 1938).

The Legacy of Israel (Oxford, 1928).

LIETZMANN, Hans, *The Beginnings of the Christian Church* (second edition, London, 1949).

MEECHAM, H. G., *Light from Ancient Letters* (London, 1923).

MILLIGAN, George, *Selections from the Greek Papyri* (Cambridge, 1910).

MOORMAN, J. R. H., *Church Life in England in the Thirteenth Century* (Cambridge, 1948).

MOULE, C. F. D., *The Language of the New Testament* (Cambridge, 1952).

MOULTON, H. H., *A Grammar of New Testament Greek*, vol. i. *Prolegomena* (third edition, Edinburgh, 1908).

New Sayings of Jesus and Fragments of a Lost Gospel, edited by B. P. Grenfell and A. S. Hunt (London, 1904).

New Gospel Fragments (British Museum, 1951).

OESTERLEY, W. O. E., *Ecclesiasticus* (Cambridge, 1912).
The *Wisdom of Ben Sira* (London, 1916).
PAYNE, Robert, *The Fathers of the Western Church* (London, 1952).
PFEIFFER, R., *Introduction to the Old Testament* (London, 1948).
QUILLER-COUCH, Sir A. T., *On the Art of Writing* (pocket edition, Cambridge, 1923).
ROBERTS, Bleddyn J., *The Old Testament Text and Versions* (Cardiff, University of Wales Press, 1951).
The *Hebrew Scrolls from 'Ain Feshka*, article in *Religion in Education* (Autumn, 1949).
ROBINSON, H. Wheeler, ed. *Record and Revelation* (Oxford, 1938).
ed. *The Bible in Its English and Ancient Versions* (Oxford, 1940).
ROTH, Cecil, chapter in *Cambridge Medieval History*, vol. vii.
ROWLEY, H. H., *The Covenanters of Damascus and the Dead Sea Scrolls* (Manchester, 1953).
The *Historical Background of the Dead Sea Scrolls* (article in *Expository Times*, September, 1952).
ed. *The Old Testament and Modern Study* (Oxford, 1951).
Sayings of Our Lord, edited B. P. Grenfell and A. S. Hunt (London, 1897).
SEEBOHM, Frederic, *The Oxford Reformers* (Everyman Library edition, 1914).
SOMMER, H. Dupont, *The Dead Sea Scrolls* (Oxford, 1952).
SOUTER, Alexander, *The Text and Canon of the New Testament* (London, 1925).
STENTON, Sir F. M., *Anglo-Saxon England* (second edition, Oxford, 1947).
STREETER, B. H., *The Four Gospels, A Study of Origins* (London, 1924).
SWETE, H. B., *An Introduction to the Old Testament in Greek* (Cambridge, 1900).
SYMONDS, J. A., *Renaissance in Italy* (London, 1900).
TAYLOR, Vincent, *The Gospel according to St. Mark* (London, 1952).

THACKERAY, H. St. J., *The Letter of Aristeas* (London, 1917).

TORREY, C. C., *The Four Gospels, A New Translation* (New York and London, n.d.).

Two Biblical Papyri, edited C. H. Roberts (Manchester, 1936).

UNDERHILL, Evelyn, introduction to *The Fire of Love* and *The Mending of Life*, by Richard Rolle, edited C. C. Comper (London, second edition, 1920).

An Unpublished Fragment of the Fourth Gospel, edited C. H. Roberts (Manchester, 1935).

WESTCOTT, B. F., *History of the English Bible* (second edition, London, 1872).

Some Lessons of the Revised Version (fourth edition, London, 1903).

WESTCOTT, B. F., and HORT, F. J. A., *New Testament in the Original Greek*, Introduction (Cambridge and London, 1882).

INDEX